JONATHAN MAYO

FACING CLEMENS

HITTERS ON CONFRONTING BASEBALL'S MOST INTIMIDATING PITCHER

WITH A FOREWORD BY ROGER CLEMENS

THE LYONS PRESS
GUILFORD, CONNECTICUT
AN IMPRINT OF THE GLOBE PEQUOT PRESS

For SARA
Who inspires me daily to become a better person

The Lyons Press is an imprint of The Globe Pequot Press.

Library of Congress Cataloging-in-Publication Data

Mayo, Jonathan L.
  Facing Clemens : hitters on confronting baseball's most intimidating pitcher / Jonathan Mayo.
     p. cm.
  ISBN 978-1-59921-162-6
  1. Clemens, Roger. 2. Baseball players--United States. 3. Pitchers (Baseball)--United States. 4. Baseball players--United States--Anecdotes. I. Title.
  GV865.C4384M39 2008
  796.357092--dc22
  [B]   2007049967

Printed in the United States of America

10 9 8 7 6 5 4 3 2 1

CONTENTS

FOREWORD

OVER MY TWENTY-FOUR YEARS PITCHING in the major leagues, I have faced a lot of batters, including the ones you will read about in this book. I may have been fortunate to pitch for twenty-four years, but it has been no accident. I have adjusted throughout my career—to the height of the pitchers mound, to the size of the strike zone, to the different ballparks. And, of course, I have had to adjust to different hitters. Each one is a challenge. If I had not adjusted, you would not be reading about me now.

I take pride in stating that I am a *power pitcher*—with emphasis on both words. Still, I have to adjust from game to game to what is working for me, and to the hitters I am facing. My goal is to make hitters feel uncomfortable. After all, they are trying to get a hit and I want them to make an out. So even if they are my friends, the game is no time for friendship to be on display.

I love to face power hitters. Don't go to the concession stand when that is happening. It is time for pitcher and hitter to air it out. Contact hitters are more difficult, because they run up the pitch count. I think pitch count is overrated these days, but every team tracks it, so it is reality.

I learned how to pitch in Fenway Park—what a great place to pitch, with fanatical fans. But Minute Maid Park in Houston is tougher than Fenway, because there is no "Monster" over the Crawford boxes. Speaking of Fenway Park, I have good recollections of playing long catch in the outfield with my son, Koby, and Tony Pena Jr., son of my then-catcher with the Red Sox, Tony Sr. Now I don't want to sound old, but I just faced Tony Pena Jr., now the shortstop with Kansas City. And my Yankees first base coach is Tony Pena Sr. Father Time has been good to me, but he reminds me constantly of how old I am getting.

Speaking of father-son relationships, I remember going to the Caribbean on a charity trip with Ken Griffey Sr. He had a teenage kid with him who played video games night and day in the lobby of the hotel. I knew then the kid had good hand-eye coordination. A few years later, when Junior was in the big leagues and my two older boys were eight and seven, he would tell them, "If you get your dad to give me some good pitches, I will get you some Nintendo games." Well, you can believe that my sons were so eager to get those video games that they came to me all open-mouthed begging for me to help Junior so they could get the free games. I had to tell them, "Stay away from that man."

Speaking of kids with the right stuff, when I was at the opening of a Planet Hollywood, a seventeen-year-old came up to me to introduce himself. He was very cordial and made a good impression. I was told later that he was the best player in Miami. Oh yeah, his name was...Alex Rodriguez, now my teammate with the Yankees with over 500 home runs.

It has been a great ride. I loved facing Reggie Jackson, Robin Yount, George Brett, shoot, every single hitter. I guess when I retire I will reflect more on how much fun all this work has been. I would have loved to pitch to Yogi Berra and Johnny Bench. That would have been too good.

Jonathan Mayo will take you on a journey to see what it is like to face me through the eyes of some of the best hitters in baseball, and also through the eyes of my son, Koby. I hope you enjoy the journey.

—Roger Clemens

ACKNOWLEDGMENTS

WHEN TAKING ON THE TASK of writing your first book, you better have a tremendous support system in place. I can't even imagine setting off on this journey without the unwavering help and assistance of my family.

First, my mother has been an everlasting source of encouragement throughout my life. She's been a role model, both personally and professionally as a well-published author, a friend, a confidante, and, most central to this project, a copy editor.

This work would never have been completed if it weren't for my wife, Sara. Some would argue, and they would be right, that perhaps it wouldn't have been started. I've contemplated the abstract concept of writing a book for quite some time, but it was her push that got me going and it was her understanding that gave me the time and space to finish what I started.

My children, Ziv and Elena, didn't totally comprehend what it was I was doing, but talked in hushed tones about Daddy working "on his book." My son's love of baseball grows exponentially by the day and he did have some grasp of the subject matter. After frequently allowing me to get my work done, I look forward to them being able to read these pages in the future.

Researching the hundreds of games and at bats discussed in this book was no easy task. It would have been impossible without the fine work of the folks at Retrosheet.org. Retrosheet president David Smith's assistance in pinpointing specific Clemens-related statistics proved to be invaluable.

There would be no story to tell without the major-league hitters, past, present, and future, who were willing to talk with me at length about what their experiences facing Clemens were like. Each and every player featured in this work was generous with his time and memories of digging in against the Rocket. Special thanks in setting up these interviews go to Chuck Berry, Mike Dillon, Brian Goldberg, Brad Hainje, John Maroon, Josh Rawitch, Andy Shaw, Jim Trdinich, and particularly to Randy Hendricks, who not only assisted in getting Koby Clemens for the final chapter but also signed up Roger Clemens to write the foreword.

Any rookie needs good coaching during his debut. Thanks to my editor Rob Kirkpatrick and Stacey Glick, my agent, for guiding me through this process. And finally, I'd like to thank Roger Clemens. Without such a thrilling, varied, and exciting career, after all, there would be no book to write.

INTRODUCTION

BASEBALL IS A SPORT THAT lends itself to statistics. It's easy to look up who has the most home runs of all time, who won the batting title in 1957, and who has the single-season record for saves. The world of baseball statistics has evolved so much, become so specialized, that you can easily find a player's career WHIP (walks + hits divided by innings pitched), his OPS (on-base plus slugging percentage), or his adjusted ERA (earned run average) with a few clicks of the mouse. So when the discussion of the best pitchers of all time comes up, it's easy to turn to numbers to back an argument. Perhaps those figures don't travel well across generations and different eras of the game, but on a base level, an ERA is an ERA regardless of when a pitcher posted it.

What do the numbers say about the subject of this book, Roger Clemens? At the conclusion of the 2007 season, Clemens was eighth on the all-time list in wins, with just one pitcher whose career was post-1940 ahead of him: Warren Spahn. The Rocket is first on the all-time active list in this category, with only Greg Maddux remotely close to him. He reached 350 wins with the second fewest losses in the game's history, behind only Cy Young.

Wins, of course, can be misleading because they are so often not within a pitcher's control. Clemens is second all time in strikeouts and his name can be found on career leaderboards in a host of categories from things that show off his longevity, like games started or innings pitched; to his dominance, like shutouts; or to "new-fangled" stats like adjusted ERA+, which measures a pitcher's ERA against the league average with ballpark effects taken into account. A stat like that helps bridge the generational divide for a "greatest pitcher of all time" debate. When stacked against his contemporaries, it almost isn't fair. Clemens leads just about every active career statistical list.

Of course you can't figure out where to put Clemens in a historical context without discussing his unmatched seven Cy Young Awards, his Most Valuable Player Award, his eleven All-Star Game invitations, his two World Series rings, and his four other Fall Classic appearances. Using other metrics to get a sense of his greatness can help. Bill James created measurements like the Black Ink Test, which looks at how often a player led a league in "important" stats, and the Grey Ink Test, which counts top 10 finishes in the same categories. In the Black Ink Test, Clemens has scored a 100, putting him fifth all time among pitchers, tied with Cy Young. With Grey Ink he got a 314, eighth all time. By the way, the average Hall of Fame pitcher comes up with a 40 and 185, for those of you scoring at home.

Speaking of the Hall, there are indices, based on more Bill James work, that help measure a player's worth or likelihood of gaining entrance into Cooperstown. A likely Hall of Famer scores around a 50 on the Hall of Fame Career Standards Test according to the site baseball-reference.com. Clemens scores a 73, the fifth-best mark, right behind Grover Cleveland Alexander. Then there's the Hall of Fame Monitor, which measures how likely a player is to gain entrance—not necessarily how deserving—into Cooperstown. A score of 100 means it's likely, 130 is almost a guarantee. Clemens scores a 336, second behind only Walter Johnson among pitchers.

In the end, though, numbers only tell part of the story. To truly understand just how good Roger Clemens has been for close to two and one-half decades, it's important to go straight to those whose jobs it was to figure him out: opposing hitters. That's what *Facing Clemens* is all about. Beginning with his college career at the University of Texas and continuing through the 2007 season, this book tries to examine just what it's been like to dig in against the Rocket.

The first step was to dissect the stats—those pesky numbers again—to determine who would make a good subject for each chapter. Finding a contemporary hitter, someone who had a lengthy career that ran concurrent with much of Clemens's, seemed to be a good way to go. Just who had the most at bats against Clemens? Here are the top five players:

Player	AB
Cal Ripken Jr.	109
Paul Molitor	107
Harold Baines	105
B. J. Surhoff	104
Joe Carter	97

Ripken, now a Hall of Famer, seemed like a logical place to begin. From there it was time to look at who had success and who failed against him. Obviously, most hitters have not had a lot of luck against a pitcher like Clemens, so the idea was to find someone—preferably someone who's had a lengthy and successful big-league career—who *really* had struggled against him. In doing general research for the book, I discovered this statistical line:

AB	H	BB	SO	AVG
22	0	2	13	.000

It belonged to Twins All-Star center fielder Torii Hunter. Add three hitless playoff at bats and that brought Hunter's futility to 0 for 25. There was a nervous moment in 2007, when, thanks to Clemens's return to the Yankees, Hunter had another crack at breaking the schneid. It was hard to know what to root for. A base hit would provide an uplifting ending to the chapter. One more "0 for" would have made it a chapter about a terrific ballplayer who just couldn't scratch out that one base hit against one of the all-time greats. Hunter didn't get that base hit extending his "streak" to 0 for 28.

But what of those who've had success? They may be few and far between, but some players have gotten their share of hits. The best example has to be Mike Piazza. He's gone 8 for 19 in his regular-season career. Four of those hits have been homers. There was that big to-do during interleague play in 2000 and the ensuing chaos at the World Series, and for that reason the future Hall of Fame catcher was decidedly not interested in talking for this book. No need to fret. There were other options to choose from on this list of top Clemens hitters:

Player	AB	H	HR	RBI	BA	OBP	SLG
Jim Thome	57	21	8	17	.368	.456	.912
Ken Griffey Jr.	90	28	6	12	.311	.392	.589
Trot Nixon	35	13	3	7	.371	.476	.800
Geno Petralli	44	16	2	6	.364	.440	.545
Lou Whitaker	65	22	3	8	.338	.444	.523

Petralli is included just to show one of the great things about baseball. It's not just the stars who can excel against a particular pitcher. Some guys just have a pitcher's number. In the end, though, Junior Griffey was the most interesting subject not only because of his star power, but also because of the friendship he has forged with Clemens and Clemens's family over the years.

Once those general themes were out of the way, it made sense to hone in on specific events in Clemens's career. Why not go back awhile, before he was a superstar in MLB? He had helped the University of Texas win the College World Series back in 1983, facing the

Golden Spikes Award winner—Dave Magadan—in the championship game. The smooth-swinging lefty went on not only to face Clemens a number of times as a major leaguer himself, but also as a big-league hitting coach to teach others how to hit the Rocket.

When Clemens came onto the big-league scene, there wasn't the kind of fanfare that exists now. The Internet didn't add to the hype in 1984; all-sports networks like ESPN were really just taking root. Nevertheless, there was a definite buzz about the Red Sox first-round pick who had reached the major leagues in less than a year. When he took the mound for the first time in Cleveland that May, Julio Franco was in the starting lineup for the Indians. And he's continued to be there over the span of Clemens's career. Perhaps he's the person who knows best what it's like to stay sharp at an advanced baseball age.

Clemens has accomplished so much over the course of his career, but perhaps no single game stands out more than when he struck out twenty Seattle Mariners in 1986. Phil Bradley contributed four to the cause that night at Fenway Park, including number twenty. He echoed the sentiments of many Mariners who, while not thrilled to be dominated like that, had to admit they were glad to be there to see it happen. One of the most amazing things about that victory is that while Clemens was striking out twenty, he didn't walk a single batter. The only fact that trumps that is his duplication of that feat—20 K, 0 BB—ten years later against the Detroit Tigers.

No athlete goes through what Roger Clemens has put himself through in terms of conditioning and hard work not to win. Whatever your opinion of Clemens, there's never been any doubt about his competitive nature. That's why it made sense to feature some World Series opponents in the book. Gary Carter was the first chosen, having faced Clemens only in All-Star Game and World Series competition, at a time when players from opposite leagues would only see each other on the field in those settings. People may have a tendency to forget, due to the unbelievable ending, that it was Clemens who started the historic Game 6 of the 1986 World Series against Carter's Mets.

Clemens didn't return to the Fall Classic until 1999, his first with the New York Yankees. He'd be in three more with the Yankees after that. Chipper Jones (Braves, 1999), Darryl Hamilton (Mets, 2000), Luis Gonzalez (Diamondbacks, 2001), and Juan Pierre (Marlins, 2003) each provides unique perspectives into what it was like to step into the box against such a legend on the biggest stage the game has to offer.

I've long maintained that baseball is an heirloom, to be handed down from one generation to the next. That's true for fans, for writers, and particularly for those who play the game at the highest level. There is no doubt that Roger Clemens has touched many young players and fans, even if only by the personal example he's set with his work ethic and will to succeed. At times it's been more direct than that. Back in 2006, when Clemens was working his way through the Astros minor-league system to prepare for his return to the big leagues, he pitched in Lexington, Kentucky, in a South Atlantic League game. Johnny Drennen, a Southern California kid who'd been drafted by the Cleveland Indians just a year prior, took the Rocket deep and etched his name into history forever. Even if Drennen never reaches the big leagues, no one will ever be able to take away the fact he once hit a home run against one of the greatest pitchers the game has ever seen.

Playing third base alongside the Rocket for Lexington that day was an infielder by the name of Koby Clemens. Roger's eldest son had been drafted by the Astros the previous June, and father and son got to share the field, albeit a minor-league one, professionally for that one evening. But they've shared so much more than that, from a friendship to a hearty batter-versus-pitcher competition that has evolved over the years. All of this is detailed in what is a fitting final chapter for this book.

Numbers don't lie. They clearly show that Roger Clemens is a future Hall of Famer and one of the greatest pitchers ever to stand on a mound. But they don't show the complete truth. They don't show Clemens the competitor, Clemens the respected contemporary, Clemens the friend, Clemens the father. My hope is that, through the eyes of those who have faced him over the past twenty-five years, this book reveals at least a little of that story.

IN THE BEGINNING

DAVE **MAGADAN**

ATHLETES TALK ABOUT IT ALL THE TIME. They don't necessarily understand when it comes and goes. There are no secret formulas, superstitions, or prayers that can summon it and/or keep it going. Whenever it does arrive, though, athletes would do almost anything for it to stick around long term. Regardless of the sport, there is nothing like the feeling that you can do no wrong, when the comfort level reaches heights that can't be matched, when athletes are in…"The Zone."

No doubt you've heard it discussed. A basketball player hits ten shots in a row and he's in The Zone. A quarterback finds his receivers with pinpoint precision over an entire half or an entire game. He, too, is in that zone.

For the baseball player, The Zone comes to a hitter during a big hot streak, when the ball appears to be the size of a grapefruit or beach ball. Everything they hit is hit hard and nearly everything finds a hole or a gap for a base hit. It can last for one game or, if a hitter is lucky, a week or two.

In 1983 Dave Magadan was in The Zone for an entire season. At the time he was a junior at the University of Alabama, getting ready to embark on a professional career in Major League Baseball, first as a player and later as a hitting coach. But before all of that, he was having a record-setting season and helping the Crimson Tide make an unexpected run to the championship game of the College World Series. It was in that finale that Magadan and his teammates faced a young, slender fireballer from the University of Texas, who also would be embarking on a professional career that summer. His name? Roger Clemens.

Not that Magadan feared any pitcher at that point. All the first baseman had done was hit .525 that season to lead the nation in hitting and set a Southeastern Conference record. It's still the fifth-highest single-season batting average in NCAA history. He was an All-American, the *Baseball America* College Player of the Year, and the unanimous choice for the Golden Spikes Award, given to the top college baseball player in the nation each year. The success led the New York Mets to pick him in the second round of that year's draft.

Magadan was certainly not a complete unknown before getting to Alabama. As a high school senior, he had been a twelfth-round draft pick of the Boston Red Sox and had some family ties to the game. His uncle is longtime player and manager Lou Piniella. Even so, he never really considered forgoing his college commitment to sign with Boston. "I didn't really consider it much," Magadan said of turning pro. "I'd already committed to Alabama and thought that, physically and emotionally, I wasn't ready to be out there on my own as a professional baseball player.

College was a transition; being a college student would be a little easier. It wasn't a tough decision."

It turned out to be a good one. He hit .389 as a freshman and followed that up with a .395 sophomore campaign. The icing on the cake was that insane junior season that helped him finish with a .439 career average (still a school record and tenth on the all-time NCAA list), improve his draft status by ten rounds, and lead the Crimson Tide to the College World Series for the first time since 1950. It would be the first time the school made it to the championship game.

"It was pretty incredible," Magadan recalled. "It was just one of those places in time where everyone on the team got along great. I had a buddy of mine on the team, our third baseman, Bret Elbin. We worked equally hard on our hitting. We would throw batting practice to each other after every practice. We were pretty diligent about it. Then it got to the point where we're trying to get each other out.

"I was locked in the whole year and stayed on top of it and never really veered from our routine. He ended up having a tremendous year, too, and ended up getting drafted. I, of course, had the year I had. I was locked in every day and squared up the ball."

Alabama rolled through the postseason to get to Omaha. The Crimson Tide swept through six games, three in the Southeastern Conference Tournament and three more in the South Regional. Alabama scored 57 runs over the six games with Magadan leading the way. He went 10 for 11 and drove in 11 runs in the conference tournament. His team beat Miami, the previous year's national champions, twice in the regional. Even with the offensive outburst, Alabama managed to sneak into Omaha without too many people knowing about them.

Baseball was a tough sell at the University of Alabama in those days. The fall of 1982 had been legendary football coach Bear Bryant's final season. He passed away in January 1983, just prior to Magadan's beginning his record-setting year. Couple that with the fact the school hadn't been to Omaha in over thirty years... Suffice it to say, the Tide were big-time underdogs.

"People knew about our offense," Magadan said. "We were in the top of the nation in runs scored and batting average, but we were a bunch of no-names. We had a bunch of good ol' boys—a couple of guys from the state of Alabama, a couple of guys from the state of Texas—that nobody recruited and they ended up being great players for us. We little by little snuck up on people, this little team from the University of Alabama. 'Oh, they have a baseball team?' They knew we had a good football team, but they didn't know we had a good baseball team. It had been so long since they had had a good baseball team that nobody knew us. It all came together."

None of the teams in the field at the College World Series had faced Alabama previously, something that perhaps worked to their advantage. The Crimson Tide beat Arizona State, 6–5, in eleven innings to start things off. ASU had won the title in 1981. Magadan tied a Series record by going 5 for 5 in the game and is tied with Barry Bonds for a record eight consecutive Series hits.

Alabama then upset Michigan, perhaps the favorite with Barry Larkin and Chris Sabo on the team, 6–5. That put them in position to play the University of Texas for the first time. Both teams were 2–0 heading into the game, but Magadan would have to wait to get his licks against Clemens.

The Rocket had started the game on June 6, the day before Alabama beat Michigan. He gave up 7 hits and struck out 12 over 8⅔ innings, but got a no-decision when Oklahoma State tied the game up in the ninth. The Longhorns went on to win the game, 6–5, in extra innings. By then Clemens was no stranger to College World Series success. He had thrown a five-hitter against Oklahoma State just one year prior, in 1982. He tossed thirty-five consecutive scoreless innings in the postseason that year, helping Texas finish tied for third in the nation. But he would sit and watch as Texas ended Alabama's fifteen-game winning streak in a 6–4, ten-inning game.

"The first game, they threw a left-hander against us because we had some good left-handed hitters on our team and it actually worked," Magadan recalled. "It kind of neutralized our lineup and we ended up losing. Then they came back with Clemens in the last game."

To get another chance at Texas, Alabama had to beat Arizona State again, and this time the Crimson Tide blanked the Sun Devils, 6–0. Texas, meanwhile, bounced Michigan from the tournament with a 4–2 win to set up a rematch, with Clemens on the mound.

Clemens led the Longhorns staff in innings pitched with 166 and strikeouts with 153 in 1983, all while finishing among the nation's leaders in wins with 13 and a 3.04 ERA. But the amazing thing to consider is that Clemens wasn't even the best pitcher on his team that year. That honor belonged to Calvin Schiraldi on a staff that led the nation with a 2.72 combined ERA. Schiraldi went 14–2 in 1983, with a miniscule 1.74 ERA.

Back then, Major League Baseball's draft took place during the College World Series and there were scouts all over the Series trying to get last looks on the various draft-eligible players in Omaha. The draft took place on June 6, the same day Clemens struck out a dozen Oklahoma State batters, and Schiraldi was getting as much, if not more, attention from scouts. The Mets took Schiraldi with the twenty-seventh overall pick, while Clemens went nineteenth overall to the Boston Red Sox. Magadan, for his part, went in the second round to become Schiraldi's teammate in the Mets organization.

"Roger kind of had an off year, if you can imagine that," Magadan said. "His ERA might have been over 3.00. Schiraldi was the one who really dominated. Obviously, both of those guys impressed me. Schiraldi was the guy who put up the big numbers that year and Roger didn't pitch up to expectations. Once Roger ended up getting drafted and dominating in his first year of pro ball, it kind of threw that out the window. They were probably a little disappointed in the way Roger threw that year and pleasantly surprised with Calvin."

While it was Schiraldi who made the Series all-tournament team, it was Clemens with the ball in his hand for what would be his final college start and a chance to give Texas its first Series title since 1975. Even if Clemens was the number two starter, Magadan and his teammates knew they had their work cut out for them. In past seasons Magadan may have wondered going in if he was up to the task. There certainly were a fair share of good arms in his home Southeastern Conference, but there was always a sense of lowered expectations from Alabama and its baseball program.

After his sophomore year, though, Magadan headed to Alaska to play in the elite summer league there. It was the first time Magadan's horizons were broadened in terms of opposition. He got to see a lot of top-flight arms from areas outside the Southeast region he really hadn't left in two years of college ball. "I gained a lot of confidence playing in the Alaska League that summer," Magadan recalled. "I faced a lot of guys from other parts of the country. It was such a great experience facing guys I had read about and had a lot of respect for. It was the same thing with Roger. We knew we had our work cut out for us going into the game against him. It was going to be a challenge."

The challenge, for Magadan, at least, wasn't going to be the Clemens fastball. His time in Alaska enabled him to see a steady diet of pitchers who could throw as hard as Clemens did. The Rocket wasn't going to beat the top college hitter in the game with heat. "Not that he was any slouch, but it wasn't like he was going to just blow us away with his fast-ball," Magadan said. "We were kind of expecting that he was going to have a good fastball."

They weren't ready, however, for how good his curve was going to be. Even at the top college level, the number of pitchers who had plus breaking stuff and the ability to command it could be counted on one hand. That's what made Clemens special, at least on that day in Omaha. "It was the other stuff, the break of his breaking ball, the tight rotation of it, it's something that sticks in my mind," Magadan said. "The velocity was there, too, but you see that maybe from three or four guys, so you get a little more accustomed to it. It was that breaking ball that really stands out."

And it was that breaking ball Magadan couldn't hit. He wouldn't be the first or the last player to have trouble figuring out Roger Clemens, but few pitchers completely dominated Magadan in the spring of 1983. And he almost never carried his bat back to the dugout. Up to that point Magadan had struck out just six times all season. But Clemens got him twice in that one game.

"I remember he threw me a breaking ball and I swung through it. He actually struck me out the first couple of at bats," Magadan said. "I remember one of the strikeouts was on a breaking ball, and I can remember I thought to myself, 'I've never seen a breaking ball like that, that good.' I can remember it like it was yesterday."

Alabama actually held a 2–0 lead against Clemens and Texas until the sixth inning. The Longhorns scored four times in the sixth and seventh to take a 4–2 lead. That held into the ninth when Magadan strode to the plate to lead off the Crimson Tide's final chance. He finally did manage to pick up one base hit off Clemens, in that final at bat. He came around to score after his leadoff double to bring Alabama to within a run, but Clemens shut the door and the Longhorns celebrated their first championship in thirteen years. Texas became the tenth team to go undefeated in College World Series play. Magadan remembers that, while it may be a two-base hit in the box score, there was more good fortune than skill involved in his rally starter.

"I had two strikes on me in every at bat," said Magadan, who finished with a .550 Series average and was the first baseman on the all-tournament team. "I got a cheap hit off of him. I was lucky. He threw me a breaking ball, I hit it off the end of the bat and looped it into right-center. I was just impressed with the total package of mound presence, the way he just took control of the game. I can vividly remember the stuff that he had, it was the best stuff I had seen up until that point."

Magadan knew it was big-league caliber stuff, without question. With Clemens taken just thirteen picks in front of him, Magadan understood both were headed in the same direction. If he wanted another crack at the Rocket, it would have to be on baseball's largest stage. "I knew he had been drafted in the first round; I certainly thought, or hoped, I'd at some point get to play him because I knew he was a major-league pitcher," Magadan said. "That was my sense of it. I figured if I was going to face him again, it was going to be in the big leagues, and that was all right with me."

It would take a decade for the rematch to occur in Boston. Clemens made a beeline to the majors, spending less than a year in the minor leagues before hitting Fenway Park in 1984. Magadan worked his way through the Mets system a little more slowly, though he hit every step of the way. He got his first taste of New York at the very end of the team's 1986 championship season and brought a .323 career minor-league average with him. The Mets would face Clemens in the World Series that fall, but Magadan watched that matchup from home.

"We were the castoffs. We were September call-ups," Magadan said of his big-league debut. "They [the Mets regulars] kind of dominated the league the whole season and all of a sudden, we're twenty-two-, twenty-three-year-old rookies there, basking in the glow of what they accomplished for five months. At times it felt like we were outsiders. They had a job to do. They really didn't want us sticking around for the postseason."

The Mets clinched the National League East early that year, on September 17. Magadan got the start at first base, giving Keith Hernandez some rest, on clinching day. Other than that, Magadan and the other call-ups could take pride in competing well when they did get the chance to play and provide their main contribution to the team: letting the veterans catch their breath and get ready for the playoffs. It may seem like a small contribution, but it helped

Magadan feel a little bit more like he belonged, at least for that one game.

"It did help. It gave me a sense, at least I contributed a little bit, especially to the celebration that night," Magadan said. "What we did was give them some opportunities to take some days off and rest up for the postseason. It was a strange feeling, something I'd never experienced before. You get your call-up like that and I had a lot of success right away, but at the same time, you feel like it was somebody else's party and you were just hanging out."

So Magadan headed home and watched his Mets forge a path to the Fall Classic. Boston was doing the same in the American League, with Clemens already established as the best pitcher in the junior circuit. Very few of the Mets had any experience in facing Clemens. Gary Carter saw him that July in the All-Star Game, but that was about it. Ironically, the kid who went home at the end of the regular season had more of a history against Clemens than the players who dug in against him twice in the World Series, not that they would've asked him for any kind of scouting report. "I doubt if any of them even knew I had faced him," Magadan said. "It was a proud bunch of veterans, some real students of the game. I'm sure they watched enough video that they had a pretty good idea what Roger was going to do to them."

It was a little surreal for Magadan watching Clemens on the mound competing against the Mets. After all, it had been just three years since the two had done battle on college's largest stage. He'd been

following Clemens's quick career path, and every success Clemens had early on gave Magadan a little
more confidence that he would one day join him as
an established major leaguer.

"It was a little bit strange," Magadan said. "It
was a kind of badge of honor, being able to tell my
buddies, 'Yeah, we faced him a couple of years ago at
the College World Series.' Especially one of the guys
on our team, Bee Smith, our right fielder, hit a home
run, almost hit two home runs off of him. He could
certainly brag about that.

"I kept track of Clemens. I knew how he was
doing after he got drafted and the way he dominated
baseball that first half-season of pro ball and he
ended up getting to the big leagues pretty quick. It
kind of gives you the idea that maybe I have a chance
to make it. I faced this guy. I got drafted pretty high
in the same draft. Maybe I have a shot."

Magadan would finally have another shot at facing his College World Series nemesis seven years after
that '86 Fall Classic. Following the 1992 season Magadan left the Mets and signed a free agent deal with
the Florida Marlins. They dealt him to the Seattle
Mariners at the end of June 1993. At the time, Seattle
was still in the AL West race, 4½ games behind the
White Sox. Magadan would hit .259 the rest of the
year and the M's would finish in fourth place, 9½
games out.

When Magadan met Clemens for the first time as
a big leaguer—on July 16—his Mariners were tied for
fourth, but only three games behind the eventual division winners, the White Sox. The Red Sox were also

only three games back in the AL East, in fifth place behind the Blue Jays. So much was still possible.

Clemens was making his first start in nearly a month. A strained groin muscle put him on the disabled list from June 21 until July 16. He'd also end up missing the final two weeks of the season with an elbow problem and was held under thirty starts and 200 innings for the first time since 1985. He'd finish the year 11–14 with a 4.46 ERA, the first time in his career he had a losing record.

When he took the mound at Fenway Park for his first start back against Magadan and the Mariners, none of that seemed to matter. The Rocket went six innings that night, allowing just 4 hits, 1 run, and 2 walks, while striking out 6. Magadan started at third base for Seattle, hitting seventh, and singled with two outs in the top of the second inning. That would seem uneventful except for the fact it would be his only base hit in twelve at bats against Clemens.

"Of course, he pitched pretty well against us and got the win and all that good stuff," said Magadan, who flied out twice to left field in his other two ABs versus Clemens in that game. "He was impressive. The one thing I always remember about facing him was his mound presence. He just owned the ballpark when he was on the mound. Even today, he's the same way."

He wasn't the same way the rest of that year, as Clemens went 3–8 before shutting it down. Both teams fell out of contention and Magadan headed back to the National League for the next three seasons. The Mariners traded him back to the Marlins, where he spent the 1994 season. In 1995 he played for the Houston Astros, then made the Chicago Cubs his home in 1996. Magadan made the one-year free-agent contract an art form, playing with four separate teams in four years. That fourth year, in 1997, he came back to the American League to play for the Oakland A's and actually spent two seasons in the junior circuit (though he played in only thirty-five games in 1998).

Coming to Oakland four years later gave Magadan another crack at Clemens. The 1997 season was Clemens's first with the Toronto Blue Jays, having signed as a free agent during that previous off-season. Oakland and Toronto met at the end of May in Oakland, then followed that up with a series north of the border in Toronto. Clemens pitched twice in those series during a season that saw him return to Cy Young Award form. He went a combined sixteen innings, allowing 2 runs on 13 hits, walking 5, while striking out 12. He won both outings to run his record to 11–0. He wouldn't lose his first start until the next one, on June 11.

Clemens's ability to reinvent himself during his time in Toronto is remarkable. The biggest thing, of course, was his development of a split-fingered fastball. If he could no longer rear back and throw it by people all the time—he still had and has the ability to do that when needed on occasion—he'd learn new ways of getting hitters out.

Magadan faced him just twice during that 1997 season, grounding out once in each game. He was the starting third baseman on May 2, 1998, when

Clemens tossed seven innings of one-hit ball at the beginning stages of another Cy season, and he grounded out three times against the Rocket. Two starts later, the Blue Jays were in Oakland and again Magadan was the starter at third. The A's actually managed to win that one, though Clemens allowed just 1 earned run over eight innings (he walked 6 and struck out 9). Magadan went 0 for 4 in the game, striking out in his second at bat against Clemens. That's noteworthy because, despite only going 1 for 12 against Clemens in his career, that was the one and only time Magadan brought the bat back to the dugout against him.

"That's what made him, put him over the top, how he was able to get better and better as he got older and older," said Magadan who, it should be noted, walked (718) more times than he struck out (546) in his big-league career. "He didn't just rely on the same repertoire as he was getting into his thirties. He developed the split, started throwing a cutter, he'd two-seam the ball. He could always reach back for that 95–96, even at forty-one, forty-two years old. He learned some other tricks and some things to help him get through those tough innings without having to rely on that fastball. That's what's made him as great as he is, that he was able to do that.

"That's what he developed the last eight or nine years," Magadan continued about the splitty. "He could control it by how spread his fingers were. If the fingers were spread just a little bit, it would have action like a sinker. Or he would really jam it between his fingers and throw it straight down to strike somebody out. What a weapon!"

He was able to continue using that weapon long past the point when Magadan had hung them up as a player and had moved on to his coaching career. His last big-league at bat came in 2001 for San Diego and he became the organization's roving minor-league hitting instructor the following year. In 2003 he was back in the big leagues as the Padres hitting coach. Just when he thought the book on him versus Roger Clemens was closed, Clemens signed a free agent deal with the Astros. Now, suddenly, Magadan would have to figure out a way to teach Padres hitters how to hit Clemens, seven years after having faced him for the final time.

"We didn't have an advance scout for most of the time I was there, so all of the advanced scouting was done by me," said Magadan, who held the job with San Diego until June of 2006. "I looked at video of whoever we were facing, of his last four starts, I would type up an advanced scout report, how I thought we should attack him."

There's no easy answer to that question when it came to Clemens. He would win Cy Young Award number seven in his first season in the National League, and he finished third in the voting the following year. In other words no one really hit him that well while he toiled for the Astros.

In 2004 Clemens faced Magadan's troops twice and allowed just 3 earned runs over fourteen innings. All of baseball hit just .217 against him and the Pads helped bring down that average by managing just a .152 batting average against Clemens. He was even more stingy in 2005, allowing a baseball-wide .198

batting average against. He actually lost his one start against San Diego, but yielded just a .185 batting average and 2 runs over eight innings.

"Every once in a while, you come up with a pitcher, I'm looking at him and thinking, 'What are we going to do?'" Magadan confessed. "You have to get his fastball down, but you have to get his split up. Easier said than done. You can tell guys, keep a good approach, stay up the middle with him, it'll help you stay on the split, try not to cheat."

All the words of advice, when facing a pitcher the caliber of Roger Clemens, might end up being useless. When Clemens is on his game, as he has been more often than not throughout his career, a hitter's approach doesn't really matter. Once Clemens became a more complete pitcher, hitters weren't left with much hope of success. That's why Magadan thinks Clemens belongs at number one in any discussion of greatest pitchers in Major League Baseball history. "I would have to say at the top of the heap," Magadan said. "He could get you out in so many ways. He struck me out one time, I probably faced him twelve times. I only have one hit. He got me out in so many different ways.

"The time he struck me out, he blew me out upstairs with a high fastball. A lot of the times he got me out with the split. It wasn't a strikeout splitter; it was almost like a two-seamer that you hit off the end of the bat. Or a high, up-and-in fastball that jams you. He just got me out a lot of different ways. I usually had success against power pitchers. I liked guys who threw hard, but he wasn't like that. He was a power pitcher who could pitch and that's what made him tough."

JULIO **FRANCO**

WHEN ROGER CLEMENS BEGAN his major-league career on May 15, 1984, in Cleveland, Ronald Reagan was finishing up his first term as president of the United States. The number one song in the country was Lionel Richie's "Hello." Somewhat fittingly, *The Natural* had opened in movie theaters the previous weekend.

Nearly all of the players involved in that game are long since out of baseball. One, Wade Boggs, is in the Hall of Fame. Others, like Mike Hargrove at the big-league level and Brett Butler in the minor leagues, went on to sit in dugouts as managers. As of the 2007 season, just one other player, along with Roger Clemens, still put on his uniform as an active player. This baseball senior citizen, perhaps more than anyone else, has a grasp of what Clemens has accomplished by being that good for that long.

"Believe me, I know," said Julio Franco, who turned forty-nine during the 2007 season, the twenty-third campaign he'd had at least one at bat in the big leagues. "I know how much preparation; I know how much we have to prepare ourselves mentally and physically with all the aches and pains to continue playing at this age. If there's someone who knows, I know."

Before beginning a quest to play until he's fifty years old and becoming the oldest regular position player in Major League Baseball history, before he became a pinch hitter extraordinaire, before he used baseball as a passport to play professionally in Mexico, Japan, and Korea, Julio Cesar Franco was a Rookie of the Year candidate, a batting title contender, and an All-Star infielder. When he was in the lineup for the hapless Indians in the middle of May in that 1984 season, he was just at the beginning stages, establishing himself as a productive big-league hitter.

The May meeting at Municipal Stadium almost didn't happen. Signed by the Philadelphia Phillies out of the Dominican Republic, Franco rose steadily through their system and made his major-league debut for the Phillies in 1982. The Phillies decided they needed outfield help following that season and packaged Franco along with a group of four other players in a controversial trade that netted Von Hayes for the Phillies. Hayes didn't live up to the kind of pressure that goes with being obtained in a four-for-one deal, though the Phillies did go to the World Series that season, and Franco set out to show his former employer they had made a serious mistake in trading away its top prospect.

He certainly did a good job of that in 1983. Franco finished second in the American League in Rookie of the Year voting to White Sox slugger Ron Kittle. The twenty-four-year-old shortstop had hit .273, driven in 80 runs, and stolen 32 bases. Kittle and his 35 home runs won the award, something Franco is not so sure would have happened had he not broken the hamate bone in his left hand in late September. The injury would require surgery in the off-season and would bother him throughout the 1984 campaign.

"They always used to talk about the sophomore jinx back then," recalled Franco, who managed to play 160 games that season. "Not any more, but it was a big deal back then. It was in the back of my mind that I had to have a good season and show them I could play the game of baseball. I was traded because they didn't think I could be successful. I thought that if I couldn't be successful, they might trade me. There was a lot of stuff going through my mind."

On May 15, he had to make room in his head for facing a fireballing phenom the Boston Red Sox had just called up to the big leagues for the first time. At the time, Boston and Cleveland were neighbors near the bottom of the American League East. The teams had finished sixth and seventh in 1983, with the Red Sox eight games ahead of the cellar-dwelling Tribe. Things weren't looking much better in 1984. With the Tigers running away and hiding atop the AL East early, Cleveland and Boston settled near the basement, already more than thirteen games out by the time Clemens took the ball for the first time. The Sox would finish ten games over .500, but eighteen games back of Detroit. The Indians would end twenty-nine games behind the Tigers, ahead of only the Milwaukee Brewers, who were then in the American League.

Clemens hadn't been in the minors for long. In less than a year after being a first-round pick out of the University of Texas, he had streaked through the Red Sox system and to Cleveland for the first of what's turned out to be more than 700 career starts. Back then, though, he was all promise and potential. There was a definite buzz surrounding him from the get-go, but the history of baseball is filled with super-prospects who don't live up to the hype. Franco saw the potential right away, but he noticed more than just arm strength and fastball velocity. Even though Clemens got the loss that night, allowing 11 hits and 4 earned runs in 5⅔ innings in front of just over 4,000 fans in Cleveland, Franco walked away impressed from his first encounter.

"There was a lot of talk about him, about the Rocket. But it was talk," said Franco, who went 1 for 3 with a run scored against Clemens in the game. "When we actually saw him, you could see there was a lot of potential. He was dominating. He had an exploding fastball.

"One thing that [separated him] from other people is that he wasn't scared. Your first time in the big leagues, you're scared even if you throw hard. But he was in command of his emotions on the mound. When you see a guy like that with a lot of talent [who] can control himself on the mound, you know he's going to be successful. For that first start everybody gets those butterflies in the stomach. But as the year went, he was in control of what he wanted to be. There are some people in life, when you see them, you see something special. Roger was one of those guys."

There's a certain rite of passage in the big leagues. No one, no matter how much potential he has, regardless how much hype there is surrounding him, can be preordained as a star or even an established

major leaguer. That kind of respect has to be earned
by everyone, the Roger Clemenses of the game included. The 1984 Indians weren't old by any stretch
of the imagination, with an average age just a touch
over twenty-seven, but the team had a number of
players with good amounts of big-league time in.
They weren't about to automatically genuflect toward Roger Clemens because he was supposed to be
the next great thing to arrive.

"You can't give a pitcher a lot of credit, especially
if he comes from the minor leagues with the background of being a top prospect," Franco said.
"Maybe he's good; maybe he's shown people he can
throw hard. You have to go to home plate thinking,
'I'm a big-league player and he's a rookie.' That's
what it is. That was the talk in the dugout, with a lot
of guys there who were veteran players. That was the
talk. He has to show me. I don't care what people
say. This is the big leagues. He's not going to come
over here and dominate like [people say]. He has to
come up here and show us, and he did."

He especially did, as Franco stated, as the year
went on. It didn't take all that long for Clemens to
start turning that "something special" into performance. He picked up his first big-league win in his
next start after facing Franco and the Indians. His
first complete game came in June, his first double-
digit strikeout total and shutout came in the same
start at the end of July. He was named the American
League pitcher of the month in August, striking out
52 in 43⅔ innings pitched, holding hitters to a .185
batting average and posting a 2.89 ERA.

Franco saw firsthand how much Clemens had learned just from his big-league debut to the end of August. Clemens tossed his second straight complete game of the month against the Indians at Fenway Park on August 26, also striking out 10 for the second consecutive outing. He started again against the Indians, this time back in Cleveland, just five days later, but only went 3⅔ innings. He had allowed just a single hit and struck out 7 when he was forced to leave with elbow soreness. It was the last outing of his rookie season as the Red Sox, far behind the Detroit Tigers, rightly erred on the side of caution. Still, with 9 wins, 126 strikeouts, and just 29 walks in 133⅓ innings, Clemens had arrived, finishing sixth in Rookie of the Year voting. Franco went a combined 1 for 6, striking out twice in their two meetings.

The 1985 season was a solid one for Franco and he played pain-free for the first time in a year. He hit .288 and drove in 90 runs for the last-place Indians. Clemens pitched effectively, but his season again was cut short. This time, it was his shoulder and it required off-season surgery. He made just fifteen starts that season, finishing with a 3.29 ERA. He had just one complete-game shutout and that came just two days past the one-year anniversary of his major-league debut. Again, the Indians were the opponent.

Franco, hitting third in the Tribe lineup, went 0 for 4 with 2 strikeouts as the Rocket tossed a five-hitter and struck out 10. It was his only double-digit strikeout game of the season.

"The first time, there were butterflies, but the second time, he was tough. He had more confidence,"

Franco said. "In three or four years, I think I knew that this guy was going to stay here for a long time just because of the way he was pitching. Every year you saw him, you could see the progress. Every time you saw him, he was walking the ladder. Every year you saw him, he was more dominating. He was more fearsome. He was striking out a lot of people. He was winning more ballgames. Every time he pitched, he was the guy who stopped a slump, the guy the team counted on: 'We've got our ace today. We're going to win today.'

"Those are the signs that you've got something special. This guy is great. It was one of those things like when Nolan Ryan was pitching. When Nolan Ryan was pitching, a lot of people got sick. Those kinds of things were happening when Roger Clemens was pitching. In the 1986, 1987, and 1988 seasons, he was the man."

In those years Clemens won two Cy Young Awards, an MVP Award, was named to two All-Star teams, topped the league in wins twice and in ERA once, finishing under 3.00 in each of the three seasons. He also took home a strikeout title and placed second the other two seasons. When he was "the man," as Franco put it, Clemens went 62–25 with a 2.80 ERA and an average of 8.83 strikeouts per nine innings.

Franco managed to miss facing Clemens in his Cy Young/MVP season of 1986. The one time the right-hander faced Cleveland—Clemens picked up his twentieth win on August 30 against the Indians at Fenway Park—Franco wasn't in the lineup. He wasn't so lucky in 1987 and 1988. In seven games against the Rocket in that two-year span, Clemens and the Red Sox won six, with the Indians finally beating him at the end of the 1988 season. Clemens threw three shutouts and even completed the one game he lost.

Franco was truly coming into his own during those seasons, hitting over .300 in each campaign and stealing 67 bases combined, 57 of those coming in 1987 and 1988. He moved across the middle infield to become a second baseman in 1988 and won the first of four straight Silver Slugger Awards as the best offensive player at the position. His numbers against Clemens in those formative years were not as pretty. He went 3 for 24 over two seasons, for a paltry .125 average. "From the 1985 season on, I felt very comfortable in establishing myself as a big-league ballplayer. By the '85 season, I was rolling," Franco said. "But it was frustrating [against Clemens]. This guy would make you uncomfortable at the plate. You knew you couldn't catch up to the fastball. Then when you were ready for the fastball, he'd throw you the curveball, so that there was no way you could see it. It was frustrating."

So was the losing in Cleveland. But Franco would soon leave that behind when he was sent to the Texas Rangers following the 1988 season. Franco won three Silver Slugger Awards his first three seasons with Texas and was named to the American League All-Star team each year. He was the All-Star Game MVP in 1990, a game Clemens attended but didn't pitch in. In 1991 they reversed roles with Clemens pitching and Franco watching from the same dugout.

From 1989 to 1991 Franco and the Rangers didn't win an AL West title, but they did finish above .500 all three seasons, a success rate Franco had not experienced previously in his career. Playing for a more competitive team helped, even against an ace like Roger Clemens. During Franco's five seasons in Texas, the Rangers faced Clemens a total of thirteen times, with Franco playing in eleven of those games. Texas went 8–3 in those eleven contests.

"The Indians were a ball club, it was a good ball club, but in the middle of May, we were twenty games out," Franco said. "It was disappointing and it was not good to play for. In Texas we had a good ball club. We were always in the hunt. You come in there and you had to beat us. It was a different atmosphere, a different attitude. There was more enthusiasm to the game. We got wins; we were playing for something. That was something we never experienced in Cleveland."

He also never experienced the buzz surrounding a marquee pitching matchup. Don't misunderstand. The Indians when Franco was there had some talented pitchers—Bert Blyleven comes quickly to mind—but none that generated the kind of attention that Nolan Ryan did when he pitched anywhere, especially in his home state of Texas. Franco and Ryan played together for the Rangers for all five of those seasons, with Ryan closing out his career in a Texas uniform. Anytime the Ryan Express took the hill was a big deal. Put him in a Texas two-step with Roger Clemens, teacher versus student, idol versus worshipper, and the excitement was palpable.

"When Nolan pitched, you had to be on your toes," Franco said. "When Nolan got to the mound, he wanted to be perfect. His mind-set was that he wanted to throw a no-hitter. If you got a hit, then he wanted to shut you out, he wanted to throw a one-hitter. I guarantee you towards the end of his career, he was fearsome. I'm sure every time Nolan pitched, Roger was watching. [You know he was thinking,] this is my inspiration. This is the guy I look up to.

"They're both from Texas and I guarantee you he gave Roger a lot of points, a lot of input: pitch this way, pitch that way, especially at the end of Nolan's career. To play in those games, you see those two guys throwing 96, 97, nasty curve balls and sliders, you don't see those things anymore, two pitchers at the same time that dominant. Now, you can see a setup man or a closer like that. But to see two pitchers of that caliber going head-to-head, it was overwhelming."

Franco got to see this matchup the first two times he faced Clemens while wearing a Rangers uniform. It was in back-to-back starts at the end of April and early May in 1989. The first matchup lived up to advanced billing, with the veteran Ryan besting the youngster Clemens, 3–1, though both went eight innings. Ryan struck out 11, pitching at home. Franco, for his part, went 1 for 4 in the game. Five days later, they went at it again, this time at Fenway Park. Neither ace was as sharp, though both pitched into the seventh inning to try to keep their teams in the game. The Red Sox scored four times in the seventh and held on to win this one, 7–6. Franco went 1 for 4 with 2 RBIs in the game, though those runs came on a double in the eighth off reliever Lee Smith as the Rangers tried to come back but fell short. In the end, though, all of that goes by the wayside. The only thing people really remember is that it was the Express versus the Rocket.

"Of course that's going to happen," Franco said. "When that happens, it's a matchup of Nolan Ryan versus Roger Clemens. And that's all that it is. I want to beat you and you want to beat me. I'm going to show you that I'm still the king in town. And I'm going to show you that I'm coming, I'm coming to take your crown. To be a part of that, it was amazing to see those guys pitch."

Franco had some of his better performances against Clemens later in that season. In two games, both big Ranger wins, the second baseman went 4 for 7 with 4 RBIs. He carried that over into the next year, with a 2 for 4 showing in their first meeting in 1990. Then came 1991. The Rangers beat Clemens twice, with Franco going 3 for 6 in the process. It'd be easy to make the claim that Clemens was still "the man" in those two years. He finished second in Cy Young Award voting and third in the MVP race in 1990 after going 21–6 with a 1.93 ERA. He followed that up by winning his third Cy Young Award in 1991 thanks to leading the AL in ERA for the second straight year and taking home his second strikeout title as well. But Franco's success against Clemens shouldn't be surprising considering the year the infielder had overall in '91.

At age thirty-two Franco had a career year. He won the batting title by hitting .341, beating Clemens's teammate Wade Boggs fairly easily. He also hit 15 home runs and stole 36 bases to win his fourth straight Silver Slugger Award and go to his third consecutive All-Star Game. "That's when I put it all together. That's when the ability caught up with the man," Franco explained. "You had a lot of natural ability, but the concentration, the focus came as you got more experience. In 1991 I put it all together and it didn't matter who pitched. Nobody could get me out. It didn't matter who was the pitcher. I realized I never hit a pitcher, I hit the baseball. The pitcher delivered the baseball, but he didn't have any control over it. It was between me and the baseball. When I realized that, I didn't care who was pitching. I had the confidence then that I had put it all together. I had the ability. I'd been in the game for a long time, now I had the experience. All I had to do was focus on winning the batting title. I was in a zone."

Franco fell out of the zone in 1992 while Clemens continued to dominate. The Rocket finished third in Cy Young voting that season and won his third straight ERA crown. To be fair, Franco's decline had nothing to do with a slump. A knee injury kept him out of all but thirty-five games that year and he hit a career low .234. Coming on the heels of his best offensive season, it was extremely hard to deal with.

"It was very frustrating," admitted Franco, who did face Clemens once that year, going 1 for 4 in a 2–1 loss in April. "Now, I know what to do. Now, I know how to go to the plate and concentrate. Then I got hurt. I missed one year with injuries. It was very disappointing to see my teammates counting on you,

you win the batting title, and the organization says, you know what, we have a second baseman that can hit. It's like you let them down. That's what I felt like."

The knee injury effectively ended his career as a middle infielder. Even in the brief time he played in 1992, he mostly was a designated hitter with a little time in the outfield and a handful of games at second. When he came back in 1993, it was as a DH only. He seemed to take to it very well, hitting .289 with 31 doubles, 14 homers, and 84 RBIs. The Rangers had their best season during Franco's tenure there, winning eighty-six games and finishing in second place behind the Chicago White Sox. Clemens faced Texas three times that year, winning two of the contests in a subpar 1993 season that saw him go 11–14 with a 4.46 ERA. Franco didn't play in one of those games but went a combined 1 for 7 in the other two.

The 1993 season would be Franco's last in Texas. He became a free agent at season's end, took a good look at the Rangers personnel, and saw the writing on the wall. Texas had Jose Canseco and they were committed to letting him get regular at bats at DH. So Franco went looking for greener pastures. He found them at Comiskey Park. "It was good for me," Franco said. "The Rangers had Jose Canseco and they chose to keep Canseco and let me go to Chicago. It was good for me because if I had stayed, I would've platooned with Canseco and I didn't want to do that."

What he did want was to play for a winner. He had gotten a taste in Texas, finishing above .500 every season he was a Ranger except for the one that was lost to him because of the knee injury. The White Sox had won the division in 1993 and Franco liked what he saw in terms of a team built for long-term success. So he signed on with excitement for the 1994 season.

It looked like a good decision. Through August 11, the White Sox were atop the American League's Central Division—the first year of the new three-division, wild card format—with a game lead over the Indians. The White Sox had a formidable lineup, with Frank Thomas hitting in front of Franco and Robin Ventura hitting behind him. Through 113 games, Thomas had 38 homers and 101 RBIs to go along with a .353 average, numbers that at least put him in Triple Crown contention. Having Franco as protection certainly helped. Franco was hitting .319 with 20 home runs and 98 RBIs, already career highs in both categories, and there was still more than a month and a half to go.

August 11 turned out to be the last day baseball was played in the 1994 season. The players went on strike and would not return until the end of April 1995. That left a lot of people asking "what if" questions about the '94 season. When the strike hit, Tony Gwynn was hitting .394. Could he have hit .400? The Montreal Expos had the best record in baseball. Could they have stayed intact longer had they won? Roger Clemens didn't finish among the first five in Cy Young Award voting, but he was second in the AL in ERA (2.85) and strikeouts (168). What kind of numbers would he have added to an already impressive resume?

No one asked more questions of that nature than Franco, whose White Sox split a pair of games against

Clemens that year. Could that have been the year he finally put a World Series ring on his finger? What kind of season would Thomas, who won the AL MVP that season, have ended with? And what kind of year would Franco have finished with? Would he have been able to do even better than his eighth place MVP finish? Unfortunately, those are all questions that will forever remain unanswered. "I went to Chicago and I had a great season. The problem was we had the strike year; it could've been one of my best seasons. It would've," Franco lamented. "Chicago was in first place at the time. Frank Thomas was hitting in front of me with 101 RBIs. It could've been something special."

Franco didn't stick around to find out if they could repeat that success. At thirty-five years of age, the veteran wasn't sure how the strike would play out and the one thing he wanted to make sure he could do was keep playing. It didn't matter where. Concerned that the strike wouldn't be settled in time for there to be any kind of 1995 season, Franco signed a two-year contract with Chiba Lotte in Japan. His $7 million contract made him the highest paid player in Japanese history. In searching for a reason why he headed to Japan and Chiba Lotte, look no farther than the manager's office. The skipper of the club was Bobby Valentine, who managed the Rangers while Franco was in Texas.

Franco wasn't foolish. Even though it was a two-year deal, he had an eye on coming back to the big leagues from the get-go. This wasn't a veteran player finishing up a fading career overseas. Franco had a solid season in Japan, hitting .306 with 10 home runs and 58 RBIs.

Major League Baseball, of course, did return in 1995, while Franco toiled overseas. Cal Ripken Jr. broke Lou Gehrig's consecutive games played streak, the first-ever wild card series were exciting, and the Atlanta Braves defeated the Cleveland Indians in the return of the World Series. What about Clemens? He went 10–5 with a 4.18 ERA in his penultimate season with the Red Sox. Franco, seeing that baseball had returned, used the escape clause built into his contract to come back and play once again for the Cleveland Indians. "I signed a two-year deal there, but it was my choice to come out of the contract. It was my choice to say yes or no," Franco explained. "I left over there. I left two and a half million dollars to come to Cleveland because I knew I wanted to come back."

One of the more valuable things he learned in Japan was how to play first base. His days as a middle infielder were long over and Franco wanted to have some defensive ability to maximize his flexibility. A player who could only DH, he knew, had somewhat limited value. But if he could play some first along with being a designated hitter, then he would have a better chance at regular playing time. He also realized that kind of situation would not present itself in Chicago, not with Frank Thomas at first base. So he rejoined the team that had allowed him to establish himself as a big-league regular.

This was not the Cleveland Indians he had left in 1988. The 1995 Tribe had gone to the World Series after winning one hundred games, losing the Series in six to the Atlanta Braves. They had a young nucleus of stars like Albert Belle, Jim Thome, Carlos Baerga, Manny Ramirez, and Kenny Lofton. Franco stepped in as the primary first baseman and hit .322 with 14 home runs and 76 RBIs in 112 games. The Indians won the AL Central again, with ninety-nine victories, but lost in the ALDS to the wild card Baltimore Orioles.

The 1996 season was Roger Clemens's last with the Boston Red Sox. The team won eighty-five games that season, but it finished in third behind the Yankees and Orioles. Clemens had what can best be termed an odd year. His 3.63 ERA was seventh lowest in the American League and he topped the junior circuit in strikeouts for the third time in his career. He also finished second in walks with 106, the only time he reached triple-digits in that category in his entire career. It wasn't the best year he had in Boston, but it also wasn't, as then-Red Sox general manager Dan Duquette said, the "twilight of his career."

Clemens signed with the Toronto Blue Jays and proved Duquette extremely wrong by winning back-to-back Cy Young Awards in 1997 and 1998. Franco obviously hadn't seen Clemens during his year in Japan and did see a slightly different pitcher in 1996 and 1997. The Indians went 2–1 against the Red Sox in games Clemens pitched in 1996. Franco played the first two games and went a combined 1 for 6. He only got one crack at Clemens in 1997, going 1 for 3, getting his only hit off Clemens while the right-hander donned a Blue Jays uniform. It was also the first time he got to see Clemens's new addition, the splitter, up close.

"He was still throwing hard, but he got smarter," Franco said. "He lost 2 or 3 miles per hour on his fastball. His velocity was down. A smart pitcher like that has all this experience throwing fastballs 93, 94, he comes with the split-finger that made him a better pitcher than he was before. He knew he couldn't rely as much on his fastball, but he had a good curveball and now the split-finger he can throw either way to righties or lefties. That's what baseball is all about, readjusting."

Franco had to readjust himself. He hit .278 for the Indians, mostly at DH, but he was released in August as Cleveland was en route to yet another AL Central crown and World Series loss. Franco, who had turned thirty-nine at the end of August, hooked up with the Milwaukee Brewers and returned to second base for the first time in years. He hit .241 the rest of the way with Milwaukee. It looked like it might be the beginning of the end for Franco.

Looks, of course, can be deceiving. Julio Franco's "Around the World Tour" began in 1998. He went back to Japan and Chiba Lotte, where opting out of his contract didn't burn any bridges. He hit .290 with 18 home runs and 77 RBIs in one season there, enough to show that there was some gas left in the tank. The expansion Tampa Bay Devil Rays were in just their second season as a major-league franchise and it seemed like they were bringing Franco in to be a veteran influence. That's not exactly how it worked out. Franco hadn't read all the fine print in his contract and before he knew it, he was being loaned to the Tigres de Quintana Roo in the Mexican League.

"Mexico wasn't my choice," Franco admitted. "I signed with Tampa Bay and the guy over there tricked me. He signed me and put a clause in the contract I didn't see. The clause said they had a contract with Mexico. He told me that if I didn't go to Mexico, they'd suspend me. So I had to go to Mexico. I didn't want to be suspended. It worked to my benefit. I told myself, 'I'm going to open some eyes. I'm going to get back to the big leagues.' "

It took a little while for those eyes to be opened, even though Franco hit .423 in ninety-three games for the Tigres in 1999. He spent the 2000 season playing for Samsung in Korea and hit .327 with 22 homers and 110 RBIs. When that didn't spark any interest, he came back to Mexico for the 2001 season and promptly peppered the league's leaderboard with his name. He led the league with a .437 average while hitting 18 homers and driving in 90 runs. He stole 15 bases for good measure, all at the age of forty-two. The Atlanta Braves finally noticed what Franco was doing. They needed a first baseman, so they brought Franco back to the big leagues. Remarkably, Franco never once worried about returning to the majors, using his faith to help guide him through his international travels.

"I'm a born-again Christian," he said. "I don't dwell on myself. I have a lot of faith in God. I always said, no matter what, if it was the will of God, I was going to come back. I won't let people dictate what's going to happen. I believed that God would renew my strength and my ability on a daily basis. I wasn't going to worry about what people were saying. I was always going to think positive."

Clemens, at the time, was going through some travels of his own. After winning his second straight Cy Young Award with the Blue Jays in 1998, while Franco was in his second tour of Japan, he was traded to the Yankees for the 1999 season. While Franco put up those gaudy numbers in Mexico, Clemens was winning a pair of World Series rings with New York. He took home his sixth Cy Young Award in 2001, the season Franco came back to the big leagues.

Franco gave the Braves a lift in September and October of 2001, hitting .300 over twenty-five games. The Braves held off the Phillies to win the NL East and it looked like they could be headed to a rematch against the New York Yankees in the World Series, having lost to New York in both the 1996 and 1999 Fall Classics. That would have given Franco the opportunity to square off against Clemens for the first time since 1997, but it was not to be. The Braves swept the Astros in the NLDS, but got steamrolled in the NLCS by the eventual World Series champions, the Arizona Diamondbacks.

Franco would have to wait until the 2004 season to dig in against Clemens in the National League. The Rocket had signed with the Houston Astros that season, his first out of the American League. Similar to Franco, he showed he had plenty left in the tank by winning his seventh Cy Young Award, pitching most of the season at age forty-one. Franco was forty-five for most of that year and hit .309 in 325 at bats. He did a lot of pinch-hitting in that season, including once against Clemens in early August, drawing a walk to lead off an inning that led to the tying run scoring, though the Astros would go on to win that game. It was an interesting way for Franco to renew acquaintances with Clemens, facing him as a pinch hitter for the first time. Not everyone can handle coming off the bench for just one at bat like that. Doing so against a pitcher of Clemens's stature makes it even more challenging.

"Off the bench, you have to concentrate on the situation," Franco explained. "What do you want to accomplish in the situation? Why are you coming off the bench to pinch-hit? Baseball dictates what you need to do. If there's a man on third base with less than two outs, you need a fly ball. If the infield is back, you need a ground ball. Other than that, you're looking for a pitch to drive.

"In a situation against Roger Clemens, it's one out of four. If you miss your pitch, that's going to be hard for you to get him because he's not going to make many mistakes with a man on third base."

The two teams met that autumn in the 2004 NLDS. Though Clemens started and won the first game of the series, Franco didn't get to face him, grounding out as a pinch hitter in the eighth inning against reliever Chad Qualls.

Franco did get his chances against Clemens in 2005. In a classic pitcher's duel in April of that year, Clemens and Tim Hudson put up zeroes. The Rocket went seven innings; Hudson went nine. Both were out of the game when Ryan Langerhans homered in the twelfth inning to give the Braves a 1–0 win. Franco started at first base in that game and went 0 for 3 with a strikeout against Clemens.

That nail-biter paled in comparison with the next time Franco had to hit against Clemens. That came in Game 4 of the NLDS that fall. Clemens had gotten knocked around a little in Game 2, going only five innings. That seemed like a positive for the Braves, but when the Astros had a chance to win the series in Houston and not go back to Atlanta for a Game 5, Clemens was up and throwing in the bullpen during a tense extra-inning affair. Franco had entered the game as a pinch hitter in the eighth inning and ended up getting five at bats. At bat number four came in the top of the sixteenth inning, the first batter Clemens faced when he came in to relieve.

"I wasn't surprised. I saw him warming up," Franco said. "If you know Roger, he's a competitive guy. In a game like this, he's going to ask for the ball. He wanted to win. I wasn't surprised to see him. I was really surprised he got the high strike call."

Franco also popped up against Clemens in the eighteenth inning, but it's that called strike three that really sticks in his craw, especially since Chris Burke homered in the bottom of the eighteenth to send the Braves home that season. "I thought the pitch was high," Franco said. "And the guy called it a strike. I was furious. I still think the pitch was high."

That would have been a dramatic ending to their two-decade long relationship as batter versus pitcher, but both refused to look at a calendar or a birth certificate. After not seeing each other in 2006, Clemens came back to the Yankees to try and help them save the 2007 season. Franco was in his second season with the Mets, acting mostly as a pinch hitter at age forty-eight. Clemens's second start back was an inter-league game and anyone who knows what New York baseball is like understands that Yankees-Mets is not a typical regular-season series. Clemens pitched in a fair share of them in his first tour with the Yanks, but this was Franco's first chance to experience it with the Rocket on the mound. The veteran got the start at first base and went 0 for 3 against Clemens, to bring his career totals against the right-hander to 19 for 94, for a .202 average.

Seeing Clemens with the Astros and then with the Yankees, Franco got a close look at what kind of pitcher the veteran right-hander had become in the many years since the last time the two met back in 1997. Just watching his 2007 debut against the Pirates on TV, Franco could tell Clemens still wasn't quite done figuring out ways to get big-league hitters out. "There was a lot of difference. He was a different pitcher, but still dominant," Franco said. "If you see him every day, he's a different pitcher. I saw him against the Pirates and he lost a couple of fastballs in the first inning. I'm sure he was a little pumped to come back against Pittsburgh. Then he settled down, starting throwing split-fingers against a young ball club. He knew he wasn't going to beat those guys throwing fastballs so he had to go to Plan B. And it worked out."

And just how much longer will it work out for both of these ageless wonders? Franco was released by the Mets in 2007, only to be picked up again by the Braves as his quest to play until he's fifty continued. Clemens still looked capable of winning big games for winning teams when healthy. Just how much further can this go? Franco isn't sure, but he's not looking at Clemens as someone he has to beat in a contest of longevity.

"He's not competition," Franco insisted. "I'm going to play until God doesn't want me to play. I'm not going to let anyone dictate when I'm going to leave the game. I play because I love this game and I think I still have the ability to put the bat on the ball, run the bases, and catch the ball. As long as God gives me that, I'm going to keep playing."

LEGENDS

CAL **RIPKEN JR.**

WHEN CAL RIPKEN JR. ARRIVED on the big-league scene full-time in 1982, Roger Clemens was still a sophomore at the University of Texas. Only separated by two years in age, they were seemingly worlds apart. Little did they know they would go on to face each other over one hundred times in careers that would collectively span more than two decades, playing in the same division for eighteen years.

Anyone who's ever watched a baseball game knows about Ripken's accomplishments. There are the 3,000 hits (3,184 to be exact), the 431 homers, the 1,695 runs batted in as he single-handedly redefined the shortstop position to pave the way for the Jeters and A-Rods of the world. Oh, and there was a fairly minor accomplishment that didn't get much attention, "The Streak," as it is commonly called. Ripken played in 2,632 consecutive games, breaking Lou Gehrig's seemingly unbreakable mark of 2,130 straight games played and then some. There's no wonder Ripken was a first-ballot Hall of Famer in 2007, being named on 98.5 percent of all ballots cast.

What most people may not realize is that over the course of his twenty-one seasons, Ripken would never strike out more than one hundred times in a season. Remember, this was a guy who barely missed an at bat for nineteen years. He passed the ninety-K plateau only twice, in the first two seasons of his career, and was over eighty strikeouts just one additional time. Clearly, he didn't carry his bat back to the dugout too frequently. In 11,551 career at bats, Ripken struck out 1,305 times. That's just one K every 8.85 at bats. It says something about Clemens that Ripken whiffed 17 times in 105 at bats, a ratio of once every 6.17 ABs.

The Streak began on May 30, 1982. Meanwhile, Clemens was helping the University of Texas go 59–6 that year, winning the Southwest Conference title. Clemens tossed four shutouts in his sophomore season, a year after joining the Longhorns from San Jacinto College. On May 30, the Longhorns were beating Eastern Michigan in the NCAA Central Regional on their way to the College World Series in Omaha. They would finish tied for third.

Ripken would hit .264 with 28 homers and 93 RBIs to easily win the American League Rookie of the Year Award in 1982. But that would be just the beginning. The following year, 1983, proved to be a big one for Ripken in the big leagues and Clemens in his final year at Texas. Ripken's Orioles would win the 1983 World Series while their twenty-one-year-old shortstop would make his first All-Star team—the first of nineteen consecutive trips to the Midsummer Classic—and be named the American League's Most Valuable Player, edging teammate Eddie Murray. He finished the year with a .318 average, 27 homers, and

102 RBIs. Meanwhile, Clemens and the Longhorns went 66–14 and won the national title. It was Clemens on the mound for the Series-winner against Dave Magadan and the University of Alabama. Just prior to winning the championship, Clemens was taken by the Boston Red Sox with the nineteenth overall pick in the 1983 draft.

It would take Clemens less than a year to reach the big leagues and it was a month into his big-league career when he and Ripken crossed paths for the first time. The Red Sox traveled to Baltimore in late June and the Orioles got their first look at the rookie phenom on June 27. Ripken was on his way to another All-Star season, hitting .304 with 27 homers and 86 RBIs.

The Orioles and Red Sox were separated by five and one-half games in the AL East at the time, but it wasn't where either wanted to be. This season belonged to the Detroit Tigers almost from the outset and they ran away with the AL East en route to winning the World Series. On June 27, they had a ten-game lead over second-place Toronto, with Baltimore 12½ games back. Still, the O's were the defending world champions and weren't to be trifled with, especially in their own ballpark.

The outing would be the eighth start of Clemens's fledgling career. The first seven, somewhat understandably, were a little uneven. The Rocket's record heading into the start in Baltimore was a pedestrian 3–1 with a 5.59 ERA. He had given up a surprising 63 hits over 48⅓ innings to that point, but he had struck out 44 and for a young fireballer, he'd shown pretty good command with just 8 walks.

The Orioles and Ripken had heard of Clemens, but it didn't go much beyond that. Back in 1984 there wasn't the proliferation of information out there at everyone's fingertips. *Baseball America* had begun publishing three years earlier, but that was about it. The Internet was barely in its embryonic stages—depending on who you want to believe—so Roger Clemens was very much a mystery when he first arrived in May of 1984.

"To me, buzz occurs when you get to the big leagues," Ripken said. "It's not like everybody who was in the big leagues was looking down the ranks. Once you do come to the big-league scene and you face somebody, you say, 'Who in the heck was that?' Certainly, he got quite a bit of attention for the success he had, so I think people knew about him a little bit more than someone who snuck up on everyone. But until you actually see him live, you don't sit in the locker room and say, 'Boy, that kid has a great arm.' Or 'He's going to be something special.' But when you hear a guy say, 'He's just plain nasty,' that's an example of the stuff he has. He had all those reactions from everybody when we first saw him."

Ripken didn't have to wait long to see just how nasty Clemens was, facing him in the bottom of the first inning with one out and a runner on first. He flew out in that at bat and Clemens retired Hall of Famer Eddie Murray to end the inning. Ripken would get his first base hit off Clemens—a single—in the third. By the end of the day, he had gone 2 for 4 with a run scored against the rookie and the Orioles would win the game, 3–1. Clemens pitched into the eighth inning, leaving shortly after Ripken scored to make it 2–0. The Rocket's line may not seem all that awe inspiring, especially when compared with future domination: 7⅓ IP, 10 hits, 3 runs (2 earned), 1 walk, 3 strikeouts. But the Orioles were certainly impressed with the young hurler's heater.

"I remember he came in his rookie season, he was blowing and pitching high in the strike zone," Ripken said. "I remember Eddie Murray saying, 'We just need to get him down in the strike zone,' and I was thinking to myself, 'That's not all we have to do, is get him down in the strike zone.' He had the ability to pitch up in the strike zone with that velocity in a place that was really hard to catch up to. He had such a live, active arm when he came in."

Clemens threw a total of 133⅓ innings in his rookie season, finishing with a 9–4 record and a 4.32 ERA, just a touch above the league average of 4.16 that season. He allowed 146 hits, one of only two times in his entire career when the hits he allowed eclipsed his innings pitched (1995 was the other). Using that high fastball, he struck out 133 American League batters and walked a miniscule 29. "The great thing about him was he had great control, which was a rare combination for a young guy. You would expect, like with Randy Johnson, for example, when he came in the league, he was pretty wild. He was working against himself with his mechanics in trying to find the strike zone. But Roger came in with his velocity and a real good understanding of control, which made him really different."

Clemens finished sixth in the American League Rookie of the Year voting, but everyone knew after that first-year performance that there was a chance he could be a pretty special pitcher. It wasn't just the sheer velocity or the explosion of the ball up in the zone. It wasn't simply fastball command. It was his mound presence and attitude that stood out at such a young age. It would prove to be the foundation of a work ethic and professionalism that has become legendary.

Clemens was just twenty-one during that 1984 campaign. Ripken played most of that year at age twenty-three, but was the seasoned veteran by comparison. He remembers how quickly Clemens got his exuberance and cockiness under wraps and started to show a tremendous amount of poise on the mound. "He was as professional as a pitcher and a serious competitor on the mound, he seemed to be unflappable," Ripken said. "Certain pitchers would be their own worst enemy. They would unravel if they gave up a jam single or somebody made an error behind them. But he was a rock of stability on the mound.

"I don't know where he figured it out so quick. He was composed, under control all the time. He was just a serious competitor. I know that some pitchers pride themselves on being a little intimidating, where they'll move you off the plate. Certainly Roger had that ability to move you back and move you off the plate, but to me, he was a consummate professional and under control at all times."

Clemens made just fifteen starts in an injury-interrupted sophomore season and none of them came against the Orioles. So Ripken had to wait another year before seeing the right-hander up close and personal again. The Clemens he did see was kind of like the Rocket V2.0. Whatever was bothering him in 1985 clearly was behind him in 1986. Clemens went 24–4 with a 2.48 ERA, striking out 238 and allowing only 179 hits en route to winning his first American League Cy Young Award unanimously. He beat out Don Mattingly to win the MVP Award as well, as his Red Sox made it to the World Series for the first time since 1975.

Clemens faced Ripken's Orioles four times during the 1986 season and it turned out to be a four-game sweep for the BoSox. While the Red Sox took over first place in the AL East on May 15 and never relinquished the lead, the Orioles finished in last place, 22½ games behind Boston. When the two teams met on June 21, Boston had a six-game lead over the second-place Yankees and the Orioles were still six games over .500 and eight games out, in third place.

Ripken went 1 for 4, driving in a run in the O's 7–2 loss in Boston. Clemens went eight in that start, yielding 6 hits and striking out a fairly pedestrian 6. But it ran his record to an untarnished 13–0. He'd improve that to 14–0 in Baltimore just six days later. Ripken actually had a pair of hits in that game, including one in the ninth that kept Clemens from getting a complete game, but he got the "W" by striking out 11 and allowing 3 runs, 2 earned, in eight-plus frames. Eddie Murray hit a pair of homers off of the Rocket in the game, evidently finally getting him to pitch down in the zone. (While Murray hit Clemens fairly well over the course of his career—14 for 40 for a .350 average—those were the only two round-trippers the switch-hitting Hall of Famer belted off of him.)

By the next time the two clubs met, on September 10 in Baltimore, the Orioles had already been officially eliminated from the AL East race and the Red Sox had an 8½ game lead over the Blue Jays. Clemens didn't have his best stuff, allowing 4 runs on 4 hits and 4 walks while striking out 6, but it was enough to improve his record to 22–4. Ripken went 0 for 3 against Clemens in the contest. The final meeting of the 1986 season, on October 1, was rather inconsequential. The Red Sox had already clinched and were prepping for the playoffs; the Orioles were playing out the string. Ripken faced Clemens only once and flew out to right as the Sox ace only went 1⅓ innings. The Sox would win that one, too, 11–7, though Ripken would go 2 for 5 with a homer over the course of the game.

Obviously, Clemens had matured even from the fairly polished professional pitcher Ripken described in his rookie season. It wasn't just one facet of his game, either. Ripken saw marked changes in just about everything the Rocket did on the mound. "He was consistent when he got to the big leagues, but he was young and still learning," said Ripken, who finished the '86 campaign with a .282 average and 25 home runs. "He just continued to get better and better.

"In 1986 his composure, his control, his consistency all went up. His ball exploded and his control inside and outside, I think he got it together in a way that he was really consistent. Maybe that was about maturing and getting his composure to a point where he was more under control. If you think back on it, though, he was pretty much under control when he got there. His ability to control the fastball and use it in many different ways, he just seemed to get incrementally better to the point where he was very consistent and he could take it out there every time."

Clemens's dominant season in 1986 also earned him his first invite to an All-Star Game. The twenty-three-year-old got the starting nod back in his hometown of Houston. It was a classic matchup of young fireballers, with Clemens starting opposite New York Mets phenom Dwight Gooden. It turned out to be a preview of the '86 World Series. Standing behind Clemens for his three innings of perfect work was a twenty-five-year-old shortstop who was happy to get a break from trying to hit Clemens.

"He started, went three innings, mowed them down, nine up, nine down," recalled Ripken about the Clemens performance that earned him the game's MVP award. "To watch that, he was pumped and he was psyched. It was his hometown; it was the Astrodome. Tony Gwynn was standing in the on-deck circle in the third inning with two outs. I remember his quotes that he wanted another chance at him because he didn't see him. Roger was on the top of his game and really throwing hard. It was fun to be on his side and not having to face that. I was glad the National Leaguers were [his victims]."

It was the first of eight times that Ripken and Clemens were All-Stars for the American League together. Usually, the Midsummer Classic isn't just a night off from facing the familiar challenges in your given league (with interleague play, of course, that rivalry between leagues has been watered down, despite the "This Time It Counts" campaign, tying victory in the All-Star Game with home-field advantage in the World Series). For a few days, at least, players can let down their guard and have some camaraderie with players who, for the rest of the season, are sworn enemies. In recent years some of those walls have been torn down and it's much more common to see opponents paling around during pregame in the regular season. Back in the 1980s, though, that was still taboo and the All-Star Game was a break from that unwritten rule.

"One of the great values of the All-Star Game is that you get the chance to be teammates with guys like Roger, just for a brief period of time," Ripken said. "If you're there a number of times, which we were able to be, you get the chance to interact with them. Sometimes—not get inside their head—but understand them as pitchers or players a little better. Hitters and the pitchers are always looking for some sort of edge."

That might have been effective with other All-Stars in any given year, but Clemens always proved to be an extremely hard nut to crack. Clemens was kind of the unofficial king of keeping other players at a distance. They may have been teammates on the AL squad for a few days, but Clemens never forgot they would go back to being adversaries in short time. Ripken made attempts over the years to get him to open up, with limited success.

"In some cases Roger wanted to be a little more aloof and not want to be drawn into the conversation since he wanted to keep the mystery about who he was on the mound," Ripken said. "I tried to draw him out a few times. Whether it was playfully wrestling around with him or one time, he was lifting his cuff weights in the training room and I came in and jumped on him and held the bottom of the table just to make it hard for him to get away. It was just trying to draw him out. I don't want to say he was standoffish, but he really understood he had to face those guys in the locker room and he wasn't going to be pals with them."

It wasn't because of a social problem or inability to interact. Instead it was a tool, something he used to gain—and maintain—a psychological advantage. And it wasn't something he was willing to let go of, even for a few days each summer. "I think it was by design," Ripken said. "He had a philosophical belief that he had to get these guys out and he didn't want to have any feelings for them when he's on the hill. He's a smart guy."

Ripken also got to see firsthand what he had heard about Clemens's work ethic. It may only have been a glimpse, but the All-Star break was anything but for Clemens. There was no time off for him, especially not from the time pitchers and catchers reported until the end of the season each year. There's a reason why he pitched well into his forties and an explanation why, save for one awful outing in 2004, he's given up just three runs in twelve career All-Star innings.

"One thing you do notice when you're a teammate of his at the All-Star Game is that the rumor about how hard he works is very true," Ripken said. "He's one of the hardest workers. You pitch only once every five days, but those other four days he's doing something; he's working out and trying to make himself better.

"The same is true when you get a glimpse of him in Spring Training. If you go see him in Spring Training, he'll pitch an inning, then he's off doing pickups or something in between innings to build his legs. Every other pitcher is sitting on the bench, gathering themselves for the next inning. Roger is different that way. Roger is one of the hardest workers that I've seen."

That work continued to pay off as the Clemens-Ripken matchups persisted beyond the All-Star Games. Clemens won his second consecutive Cy Young Award in 1987, going 20–9 with a 2.97 ERA and striking out 238 in 254 innings pitched. He completed a now-unheard-of 18 of 36 starts, leading the American League in that category as well as in shutouts with 7. The rest of the Red Sox didn't fare as well, with Boston finishing in fifth place, with a 78–84 record. The Orioles were even worse, losing ninety-five games and ending in sixth, eleven games behind the Red Sox. Ripken's average took a dive to .252, but he still hit 27 homers and drove in 98 runs for the O's. Baltimore and Boston faced each other twice and Clemens was completely dominant in both games. He completed both victories and allowed a combined total of 2 earned runs and 9 hits over the eighteen innings. Oddly, he didn't strike out a single batter in his first start, though he whiffed 9 in the second outing. Ripken didn't have much personal success in '87 versus the Rocket, either. He managed to avoid carrying the bat back to the dugout, but finished 1 for 8 with just a base hit over the two games.

The 1988 season is one Ripken would definitely rather forget. His Orioles began the season with a twenty-one-game losing streak, a record for season-opening futility, and didn't win their first game until April 28. By the time Baltimore met Boston for the first time that season, on June 18, Ripken and company were in last place with an 18–48 record, twenty-three games out of first place and thirteen games behind the team in front . . . in sixth place. The O's would finish the year with 107 losses and 34½ games out of first place, 23½ behind the sixth-place Cleveland Indians. Ripken somehow managed to have a decent individual season, even more impressive considering that his father, who had become manager in 1987, was fired after the awful start. Ripken hit .264 with 23 homers (his first full season with fewer than 25 home runs), 81 RBIs, and a career-high 102 walks (against just 69 strikeouts) for the season. Of course he made his annual trip to the All-Star Game.

Clemens joined him once again. The Rocket would finish the year with a respectable 18–12 record, and all of his peripheral numbers were terrific as usual. He led the American League with 291 strikeouts in 264 innings while walking just 64. His 2.93 ERA was good for fifth in the league. He finished sixth in Cy Young Award voting; 1988 proved to be Frank Viola's year.

The Red Sox in the early going weren't having as stellar a year. On June 18, Boston was 31–32 and 8½ games out of first all the way down in fifth place. Clemens would pitch them to .500 in Baltimore with a complete-game, 9-hit shutout. He walked 1 and struck out 9 to run his record to 10–4. Ripken went 1 for 4 with his first multi-strikeout game against Clemens. He whiffed in his first two at bats and got his base hit in the eighth, with Clemens completely in command.

The two teams met six days later in Boston, and it was a rare positive moment for the Orioles. They beat Clemens, 6–2, chasing him from the game in the third inning after he had allowed 7 hits and 6 runs (5 earned) in just 2⅓ innings of work. After the Sox moved to .500 on June 18, though, they never dipped below it again for the rest of the season. Boston moved into first place on September 4 and would hold on to win the AL East by one game for its second title in three years. The A's swept the Sox in the American League Championship Series, but it's probably safe to assume the Orioles would have loved to switch places with Boston that season.

Baltimore was determined to reverse its fortunes the following season. With basically the same roster—minus the very large presence of future Hall of Famer Eddie Murray—as the one that finished with the Orioles first one-hundred-loss season since 1954, the O's decided to have a "why not" year. Why not prove that 1988 was a distant memory? Why not get off to a good start? Why not compete for the AL East crown until the very end of the season? This is what the 1989 Orioles set out to accomplish when they began the year.

There was only one problem. Staring them down from the pitcher's mound on Opening Day in Memorial Stadium was none other than Roger Clemens. If Baltimore really was serious about turning things around, they'd have to be ready right out of the gate. "We had the greatest challenge of starting the year against Roger and the Red Sox," Ripken recalled. "He was cruising along...he struck me out. He put me away on high fastballs and I swung at them. You're all ready on Opening Day to try and reach that."

Through the first three innings, Clemens faced the minimum number of batters. The O's were able to break through with a run in the bottom of the fourth thanks to a Joe Orsulak single that scored Brady Anderson. When the Red Sox took a 3–1 lead in the sixth behind a pair of doubles and a Mike Greenwell two-run homer, it looked like the O's would have to wait at least one more day to start officially turning the ship around, especially considering how sharp Clemens looked.

Then came the bottom of the sixth inning. Anderson led off the inning with a double. After Phil Bradley walked, Orsulak moved the runners up one station with a ground out to first and up strode Ripken. At this point of his career, including the 0 for 2 he carried in the opener (he grounded into a double play in his second at bat), Ripken was hitting just 7 for 30 (.233) against the Red Sox ace. All seven hits had been of the one-base variety. "I fouled off a bunch of high fastballs and finally he threw me another one on a 2–2 count and I lined it over the left field fence for a three-run homer that put us ahead," Ripken said. "We ended up beating the Red Sox on Opening Day in a very exciting time."

The Red Sox tied up the game in the top of the seventh and the game went to extra innings. Eventually, Craig Worthington's single against Mike Smithson brought home the winning run in the eleventh inning, perhaps a sign of good things to come for the '89 O's. But without Ripken's three-run shot, his first home run against Clemens, it wouldn't have been possible.

"Running around the bases in an Opening Day environment off of someone like Roger—and Roger was blowing that day, too, he was throwing really hard and all of us were trying to catch up to him—the adrenaline is flowing as high as it can be at the start of the season," Ripken said. "Everyone is fresh and everyone is ready to go. That's a pretty good experience against Roger."

They didn't have a very good experience the second—and only other—time they faced him that season. The two teams met once again in Baltimore on August 11. By then the Orioles had already exceeded any expectations and led the AL East with a 58–54 record, two games ahead of the Toronto Blue Jays. The Sox were just half a game behind Toronto, so this Clemens-Ripken meeting had as much meaning as any previous one. Ripken and the Orioles couldn't get to Clemens as they had earlier in the season. Even though he walked 5, Clemens allowed just 3 hits and 2 runs (1 earned) while striking out 8 over seven innings. He left with a 6–2 lead and improved to 12–8 on the season after watching Lee Smith give up a couple of runs— one on a Ripken sacrifice fly—that led to a 6–4 final. Ripken went 0 for 2 against the Rocket in the game, drawing a pair of walks in four plate appearances.

That was the first game of a doubleheader and the Orioles managed to split by winning the night-cap. At the end of the night, they led the Blue Jays and Red Sox by 2½ games. What a story it would be, just a year after that 0–21 start, if the Orioles would hold on to win the AL East. Alas, it was not to be. They held onto the lead until the end of August, with Toronto meeting them atop the division on the month's final day. The Blue Jays never relinquished the lead, though the Orioles never fell further than three games back in September. Baltimore only trailed by one game when they met the Jays in Toronto for a three-game, winner-takes-all series to close out the year. They lost a heartbreaker on September 29, a 2–1 decision, in eleven innings. The O's had a lead the next day, but then saw the Jays score three times in the eighth inning to win the game and clinch the division. Ripken, of course, played in all 162 games, hitting 21 homers and driv-ing in 93 runs while finishing with a .257 average. He finished third in the American League MVP vot-ing, behind winner Robin Yount of Milwaukee and runner-up Ruben Sierra of Texas.

The Red Sox took only a one-year hiatus from the top of the division, returning to that perch again in 1990. Once again, though, they'd get bounced from the postseason by the Oakland A's after an

eighty-eight-win regular season. Clemens was phenomenal that season, going 21–6 with a 1.93 ERA
and 209 strikeouts in 228⅓ innings (he missed a few
weeks in September accounting for the slightly lower
innings total). He was an All-Star who finished second in Cy Young Award voting to twenty-seven-game
winner Bob Welch and third in the MVP race in back
of Rickey Henderson and Cecil Fielder. Ripken and
company faced Clemens twice that year, in back-to-
back starts, splitting the games. Clemens had one of
the shorter starts in his career against the Orioles on
June 18. He didn't make it out of the second inning
and it was a Ripken RBI single that chased the
Rocket from the game. When the two teams met five
days later, Clemens went nine innings and didn't
allow an earned run, but he had to wait to see the
Red Sox win the game in extra innings. In the two
games Ripken went 3 for 5 with an RBI and a walk.

The next season, 1991, was a banner one for
both Clemens and Ripken. Clemens picked up his
third Cy Young Award after going 18–10 with a 2.62
ERA. He allowed just 219 hits in 271⅓ innings that
year while walking 65 and striking out 241. He topped
the American League in strikeouts and it was the second time in three consecutive years that he also led
the junior circuit in ERA. For his efforts he'd finish
tenth in the MVP voting, even though Boston finished
in second place, seven games behind the Blue Jays.

The winner of the MVP Award that year was
none other than Cal Ripken, eight years after he had
won the award for the first time. It's a testament to
how superior a personal season it was for Ripken

that he won his second MVP Award in a year the Orioles lost ninety-five games and finished in sixth place. The 1991 season was Ripken's best, and that's saying something for a first-ballot Hall of Famer who compiled the stats he did. Ripken hit a career-high .323 in 1991. He also hit 34 homers—the only time in his career he surpassed the 30-home-run plateau— and drove in a career-best 114 runs. In 650 at bats he struck out a remarkable 46 times. Defensively, he won the first of two straight Gold Gloves. He took home the sixth of his eight Silver Slugger Awards. He even won the All-Star Game MVP. Basically, everything went right from a personal perspective.

That was even true in his matchups against Clemens. The teams again met twice and split the games with each team winning in the other's ballpark. But Ripken went 4 for 8 in the two games, even more impressive when you see Clemens's combined line in the two starts: 17 IP, 15 hits, 4 runs, 3 earned, 1 walk, and 13 strikeouts (10 of which came in the second start, a complete-game victory for Clemens). "I remember it was easier for me as a hitter when everything was going so well and I didn't worry so much," Ripken said. "When you're not hitting well, then the challenge of facing someone like Roger is way greater.

"Still, even in that year, I'd look at the paper and hope he'd pitched the day before we got to town. That's the ultimate compliment for anyone of those guys of Roger's caliber, that you hope you miss them. In the years when you're swinging well, when it becomes a challenge you feel you're armed for, you face the challenge a little bit better. When you face a great pitcher like that, he's going to get you more times than you get him. Occasionally, you are going to get him."

He didn't get him at all in 1992, the first season of Oriole Park at Camden Yards. He also didn't face him at all that year as the two never crossed paths between the lines that season. They made up for it in 1993 with four meetings, three of which were won by the Red Sox. When Clemens won the first two starts by allowing just 2 runs in seventeen innings and striking out 22, he looked like the Clemens of old. By the time the season was over, though, something wasn't quite right. Clemens missed a month of the season in June and July and finished the final two months of the season with an ERA over 7.00. For the year he had a losing record (11–14) for the first time in his career to go along with an ordinary 4.46 ERA, and he fell below the 200-inning plateau for the first time in seven seasons. Ripken who hit 24 homers and drove in 90 runs that season, went 3 for 13 against the Rocket, yet somehow managed to escape a strikeout.

The next two seasons were shortened by the baseball strike. Between 1994 and 1995 (the Red Sox won another division title in the 144-game 1995 season), Ripken would face Clemens in four games, going a combined 2 for 11 with 3 strikeouts. These were relatively lean years for Clemens. He followed up his subpar (by his standards) 1993 season by having a good 1994 campaign, finishing second in ERA and strikeouts in a season that ended in August. When he returned in 1995, he wasn't as sharp. Even though he went 10–5 and the Red Sox won yet another AL East crown, Clemens's ERA rose back up over 4.00, while his strikeout rate went down and his walk rate increased.

It was a much bigger year for Ripken, of course. On September 7, 1995, he played in his 2,131st consecutive game, breaking what many had thought was Lou Gehrig's unbreakable streak.

In 1996 things improved somewhat, with Clemens leading the American League in strikeouts and finishing the year with a 3.63 ERA. But he walked 106, the only time in his career he walked more than 100 in a season. He pitched most of that season at age thirty-three and the thinking in Boston was that he was on the downside of his career after all of those intense innings in the past decade. While history has proven that theory wrong, Ripken does recall that he wasn't quite the Clemens of old in his final seasons at Fenway.

"I remember the last few years he was with the Red Sox, and I don't know if he had some arm problems or what, his fastball came back a little bit to more of a hittable speed," said Ripken, who nonetheless went 0 for 9 with 3 strikeouts in a three-game sweep of Clemens starts in 1996 as the Orioles won the new-fangled AL wild card that year. "So his control had to be more on. He couldn't rely on just rearing back and throwing the ball past you up in the strike zone as regularly as he did before. Maybe he went through a little bit of a dead-arm period, maybe the innings he logged started to wear on him a little bit. I did notice in Boston toward the end, his fastball did come back a little bit to a normal range.

"Then, when he was in Toronto, he came back with his fastball a little and he maintained it for the rest of his career. I don't know what the situation was, but when he got to Toronto, his fastball was back. And also, he came up with the split-fingered. Maybe it was the combination of the two that made his fastball better. But I think the miles per hour came back."

Whatever the explanation, the results were very clear. Clemens, showed the door by Boston, signed with the AL East rival Blue Jays, a deal that made him the highest-paid pitcher in baseball. He certainly seemed worth it in 1997 and 1998, though it didn't reflect in the standings. Clemens won back-to-back Cy Young Awards to bring that hardware total to five. In 1997 Clemens was the winner of pitching's unofficial triple crown, leading the American League in wins, ERA, and strikeouts. He repeated the feat in 1998 to clearly reestablish himself as the best right-hander in the game. Clemens's evolution as a pitcher stems largely from a maturation process in which he realized, at age thirty-four and wearing a different uniform for the first time in his career, that he needed another pitch. It's not that he became a touch-and-feel command specialist. The power stuff never went away. But the consensus is that when Clemens started throwing that splitter, it added a whole new element that brought him back to unhittable status.

"He wasn't a finesse guy, with no changeup [when he first broke in]," Ripken explained. "He went high in the strike zone and with a breaking ball. Over time, he had a curveball that he threw every once in a while in the mid part [of the plate]. Then when he developed that split-fingered changeup, that was a really good pitch for him, midway through his career.

"It's almost like he didn't need an off-speed pitch, per se, when he was blowing and throwing high in the strike zone. But when you do have one, it makes your fastball that much better. Frank Viola came to the big leagues and had a good fastball and good curveball. He had two pitches. Bruce Hurst had two pitches and threw pretty hard. They were both lefties. But when they came up with a changeup, they went from 14–15 wins to 22 wins and Cy Young guys. When [Clemens] did come up with the split-finger in Toronto, especially with two strikes, you had to wait a little longer to determine what that pitch was, and it made everything work so much better."

While things were going well for the Orioles—they followed up their wild card performance in 1996 with their first divisional win since 1983, Ripken's first MVP season—there were signs that all those consecutive games played were starting to take their toll. Ripken had a solid year in 1997, hitting .270, but he hit just 17 homers and drove in 84 runs (after hitting 26 and driving in 102 in 1996). In 1998 that number dropped to 14 homers and he drove in just 64 runs. The two seasons were a mixed bag in terms of Clemens matchups. In 1997 Ripken went 1 for 10 against the Rocket, carrying his bat back to the dugout four times. In 1998 he went 5 for 10, including his second—and last—home run against Clemens.

But the 1998 season was much more important than picking up five hits against Clemens. This was the season that the Orioles shortstop did not have his name in the lineup for the first time in 2,632 straight games. Ripken had decided at the beginning of the season that he was going to end the streak if the Orioles fell out of the race. They finished thirty-five games behind the juggernaut Yankees of that season, so it became a question of when, not if, he'd do it.

Ripken's initial thought was to wait until the last game of the season, in Boston. Doing that, as Ripken put it, would "almost make the statement that I could've played all 162 if I wanted to." But his wife, Kelly, had a better idea. "She said, 'You know what, your last home game should be the one. Everyone's celebrated; it's been a journey. It should be a positive thing,'" Ripken recounted. "She was absolutely right. So the last home game happened to be against the Yankees, then we got on the plane and went to Toronto."

Ripken sat out on September 20, 1998, but he was back in the lineup on September 21, against the Blue Jays. His opponent on the mound that day was a fairly established right-hander. That's right, the day after the emotional roller coaster of ending The Streak, Ripken had to dig in against Roger Clemens. "I didn't know we were facing Roger," said Ripken, who went 2 for 4 in a performance that saw Clemens win his twentieth game of the season by striking out 15 over eight innings. "Just because the streak ended didn't mean you were going to dodge the challenges. One of the great things about playing every single day, the symbolism of what that means, to me, and this is really why it all happened, is that each day there's a challenge that you come to the ballpark and put yourself in the hands of the manager to almost ask if you're one of those guys who can meet that challenge.

"The challenges like Roger and Randy [Johnson] and Pedro [Martinez] and all those guys, it'd be nice to skip those guys. They can be beat every once in a while and if you're going to beat them, you have to have your best team on the field, so you have to suck it up and try to do the best you can."

Clemens's tenure in Toronto lasted only two years. After failing to make the postseason, or come close, in either season, the Blue Jays decided to ship Clemens to none other than the New York Yankees prior to the start of the 1999 season. The same Yankees that had won 114 regular-season games and swept the Padres for their second World Series title in three years. To many it just didn't seem fair.

Clemens didn't even have a particularly good first year in pinstripes, going 14–10 with a career-high 4.60 ERA, but he did get to put a ring on his finger at the end of the season, one of the few things that had eluded him in his illustrious career. While Clemens pitched well in the ALDS and World Series, Ripken points out that as dangerous as the Yankees were with the addition of Clemens, it was the whole pitching system they had that truly made them unbeatable.

"You know any place he goes, you put that caliber a pitcher in the rotation, that instantly makes everybody else better," Ripken said. "But I didn't sit down and say, 'Wow, this is an unbeatable dynasty.' We knew it was going to be tough to go in there and face those guys. I think the tough thing about that era is that they had set up their bullpen so well, to me as a right-handed hitter—and if you hit fifth or sixth, which is where I think I was hitting—by your third at bat, if it was significant it might have been the sixth or seventh inning, then you had to face [Jeff] Nelson and for your fourth at bat was against [Mariano] Rivera. It makes the matchups really difficult.

"You face the starter, you had your two at bats against them to get a chance off of them. If your third at bat comes up with a chance to hurt them, then I would always end up facing Jeff Nelson, who was the toughest of any righty who came in for those matchups. Then you'd have to face arguably the best closer of all time in Rivera. That didn't make it a real easy time to try to compete. I remember the Yankees seemed to shorten the game. They had the great starters, but they also had their matchup bullpen guys who really could do it."

The 1999 season wasn't just difficult because of facing the Yankees. With everything that Ripken had to deal with that season, trying to hit Clemens, Nelson, and Rivera was the least of his concerns. In March of that year, Ripken's father, Cal Ripken Sr., the man who raised his sons around the game as a minor-league manager and big-league coach, the man who managed his boys with the Baltimore Orioles, passed away at the age of sixty-three.

On the field it was also dispiriting for Ripken Jr. For the first time, in his eighteenth season, he landed on the disabled list. He would play in just eighty-six games and collect 332 at bats, by far the lowest totals of his career. He missed a month in May, then another month in August before his season ended in mid-September. Somewhat ironically, it was one of Ripken's better years statistically. He hit .340 and slugged .584 at the age of thirty-eight. "My back blocked up," Ripken explained. "I got a couple of shots in my back and I came back in early May. I was hitting .340 that year. In September I had the herniated disc again and that's when I went into surgery. I did it September 21 and had surgery. I had to be on my back for a while."

He did get two of those eighty-six games—both Oriole victories—and 9 of those 332 at bats against Clemens. He went 2 for 9 in those games, but it was more noteworthy what he didn't do, postsurgery. On September 30, for the first time in the sixteen seasons Clemens and Ripken were in the American League East together, Clemens was on the mound facing the Orioles and Ripken was not in the lineup.

It happened again the following season. Ripken faced Clemens in early May and went 0 for 3. But when the Orioles and Yankees met again in late July, Ripken sat and watched. For a guy used to seeing his name in the lineup every day for umpteen years, it was a tough pill to swallow. "After I had surgery and I came back, there were a lot of considerations that were uncomfortable for me: on turf, day games after night games, it was hard to get your back up and running quickly," Ripken said. "In order to play more games, sometimes you had to sit, which was a hard experience for me. It felt like you were bypassing your responsibility if you sat down against Roger or

Randy or those guys. But sometimes, the timing of that had to occur. It was a funny and bad experience. I'd much rather be in there, trying to meet that tough challenge, than sit there and watch everybody else do it."

Ripken had one last season in him, and a relatively healthy one at that. Over the course of the 2001 season, he played in 128 games, his highest total since he broke the streak back in 1998. The Orioles and Yankees played four times. Ripken didn't play in the first three meetings and the fourth and final matchup had an ending a scriptwriter would find hard to conjure up.

Before getting to that September 30 finale, Clemens and Ripken had one more Midsummer Classic to attend. They hadn't represented the American League together since 1998. Ripken, despite the slip in stats, was an automatic to be voted in. Clemens was on his way to Cy Young Award number six and got the starting nod.

The last few times Ripken went, of course, he was over at third base after years of manning shortstop. As a homage, his teammates—unbeknownst to Ripken—had planned a switcheroo. It began when starting shortstop Alex Rodriguez sidled up to Ripken and suggested an exchange. "I went out to third base," Ripken said. "I had this glove I called 'humongous'—I had Rawlings make me this bigger glove when I moved to third—and Alex comes over and says, 'Why don't you go play shortstop for an inning?' I said, 'You're out of your mind. I don't want to do that.' "

He was convinced to move when manager Joe Torre gave him the thumbs-up sign. Ripken didn't really have a choice, especially since both he and A-Rod were being recorded by MLB Productions. So he moved and gave his starting pitcher a shrug. "I kept thinking to myself, 'I must be the only one in this whole stadium who didn't know what was going on,'" Ripken laughed. "I felt I was painted into a corner a little bit. And I was miked. So was Alex. We were miked for MLB. I realized I was miked so I couldn't tell him what I really wanted to tell him.

"I begrudgingly went to shortstop and I looked at Roger, I put my hands up and said, 'I guess you're going to have to strike out the side.' He kind of laughed and smiled at me. I was thinking, 'OK, maybe I'll get an inning and won't get a play. This is a nice gesture and everything, but I've got a big glove and I don't feel like I've been over there in a while. This is not the right place to test it out again.'

"After the first batter, there was one out and I start thinking, 'OK, what's so hard about it? I can catch a ground ball and throw to first base.' So I was actually wanting the second one hit to me. I think Bonds was the third hitter in that inning. The count went to a certain count and I saw a split-finger pitch and I really started to remember how I played shortstop. I started to anticipate up the middle. He rolled over on a ball I got a great jump on. If he had hit it right past Roger, I would've caught it. But he kind of rolled over on it and the second baseman came over and made the play. But I had a really good jump on it and I was thinking, 'That've been really cool if I had a chance to make a play behind Roger.' It ended with no play and I was just as happy."

The second half of the year was basically a Cal Ripken farewell tour. He had announced his retirement in June and every time he came to a city for the final time, there was some sort of ceremony. By the time the season was winding down, Ripken was running on fumes. He had tried—and often succeeded— to do something meaningful on each stop of the tour. But by the end, both physically and emotionally, he had nothing left in the tank.

As if that wasn't enough to deal with when Ripken came to New York, this was late September 2001, less than three weeks after 9/11. The series, in fact, had been pushed back because of the tragedy. The emotional context was almost too difficult for Ripken to deal with. "By that time, emotionally, I was pretty spent," Ripken said. "Especially coming into New York, because they brought in a lot of the kids who had lost their fathers—firemen and policemen—to the ballpark and I met a bunch of them. I remember thinking they were right at my kids' ages. I was wondering how they would go the rest of their lives without their dad. And then you try to get it all back together. It was the last game in Yankee Stadium. Roger was pitching. I was trying to get all focused and concentrated because I wanted to do something good."

And he almost succeeded in his first at bat against Clemens. Leading off the second inning, Ripken saw a high fastball—the same high fastball he'd seen for the past eighteen years—that he liked and Ripken was fairly sure he got all of it. "The wind was blowing in just a little bit and it was a little colder at that time of year," Ripken remembered. "I thought I had hit it enough to go out in center field and Bernie [Williams] went back, jumped up, and caught it against the fence in center field. He didn't rob me of a home run, but he took a hit away from me."

That was the closest he got to a storybook ending. With everything going on, Ripken pressed to make something happen. Instead he struck out twice against Clemens. The game was far from over, though. Ripken ended up going 0 for 7 in the fifteen-inning contest with 4 strikeouts. The weather got nastier and nastier and with the game not having any meaning—the Yankees were playoff bound and the Orioles would be heading home—it was called with the score knotted at one.

"It got so cold and rainy and windy, it was just horrible conditions," Ripken recalled. "It ended in a tie because there were a couple of delays and it wasn't an easy game to play in. For hitting conditions it was cold and rainy and miserable. I remember leaving there saying, 'I've never left Yankee Stadium being 1–1–1.'"

And that's how their nearly two-decade relationship ended: in a tie. Doesn't seem fitting, does it? The two matched wits and skills over a hundred times and, truth be told, it wasn't a tie. Clemens, more often than not, won their battles. Ripken, a .276 career hitter, managed just a .248 average against the Rocket. One of the more difficult men to strike out over the course of his career did just that 17 times against Clemens.

When players retire, Ripken will tell you, they often take the time to really go back and relive memories with those they shared them with. Conversations with contemporaries, talking about the "old days," are commonplace. He continued to watch Clemens excel beyond his own retirement and marvel at the pitcher's ability to maintain that excellence. He's looking forward to the time when they both share the stage in Cooperstown and can sit down for a chat.

"I'd love to sit down with Roger someday and just go through it," Ripken said. "To me, Roger reminds me—I had the chance to face Nolan Ryan. When I faced Nolan in the 1985 All-Star Game for the first time, I thought, 'God, this guy has some age on him and he's still throwing as hard as anybody.' He was really blowing. He was really kind of a marvel that he can continue to go out there and work and continue to pitch all the way up until he was forty-six or forty-seven.

"Roger follows right along in the same mold. It's amazing to me the number of pitches he's thrown, as competitive as he is, as good as he is for so long. They are two remarkable people who were able to maintain their stuff throughout their careers. That's what I can remember. I had the chance to face Nolan, then seeing the whole development of Roger from the early stages to the end, those two guys are in a world by themselves."

GARY **CARTER**

BACK IN THE DAY, before the advent of interleague play and when players changed leagues much less frequently, it was possible to have a nineteen-year veteran and Hall of Famer in one league and future Hall of Famer in another, have their careers run concurrently for nine seasons, and never have the two meet in a regular-season contest.

Such is the case of Gary Carter, Hall of Fame catcher, and Roger Clemens, future Hall of Fame pitcher. So that made the times the two did meet up all the more special, though it's not difficult to dress up a pair of All-Star Game at bats and two World Series games.

None of the seven total at bats Carter had against Clemens will be found on either's regular career statistics page, nor will the fact that Carter never got a hit off Clemens, but that doesn't mean those seven separate meetings were not of the utmost importance to both men at the time.

And yes, while the World Series battle certainly trumped the All-Star Games, it's not by as much as one would think. Once upon a time, the Midsummer Classic was huge for players selected. Carter went eleven times and was named the MVP twice, in 1981 and 1984. Battling for league supremacy was the be-all and end-all for the large percentage of players who wouldn't go on to meet in the World Series. And when the 1986 All-Star Game came around, no one knew it would serve as a bit of a Fall Classic preview because of the starting pitching matchup.

When the All-Star break hit in 1986, Roger Clemens was 15–2 with a 2.48 ERA and 146 strike-outs in 145 innings pitched, making him an easy choice to get the start for the American League. It was his first All-Star appearance, the first of eleven invita-tions to the game. His National League counterpart was Dwight Gooden, the 1985 NL Cy Young Award winner. After the first half of '86, Gooden was 10–4 with a 2.77 ERA and 101 strikeouts in 136⅓ innings. Gooden, of course, had already tasted All-Star success, teaming with Fernando Valenzuela to strike out six consecutive hitters in the 1984 contest.

Not only did this game pit one young hurler, al-ready with hardware to brag about (NL Rookie of the Year in 1984, Cy in '85), against another one about to start collecting his (AL Cy Young and MVP in 1986), it was a sneak peek at Game 2 of the World Series. With everything that happened in that World Series, it's easy to forget the Gooden-Clemens duel was one of the most hyped matchups in Fall Classic history. On July 15, those who tuned in got an early glimpse.

The starters in the National League who would face Clemens didn't have much to go on. Clemens was only in his third season and had never participated in an All-Star Game or competed against any National League clubs outside of Spring Training. There weren't nearly as many games televised—ESPN had debuted just seven years prior and wouldn't strike a broadcast deal with Major League Baseball for another four— so there was more reliance on word of mouth than there might be today. Suffice it to say, there was more than a little buzz when the Texas boy came home from Boston and took the mound at the Astrodome for the first time. "He was having a very successful season. [His] starting the game was a big deal," Carter recalled. "Everybody was curious as to how hard he threw and what kind of stuff he had, what kind of movement he had on the ball. There was a curiosity more than anything."

Perhaps curiosity killed the cat in Houston that night because the National League could do nothing against the Rocket. He tossed three perfect innings, striking out a pair, to earn the win. That was saying something, considering the National League had won thirteen of the previous fourteen All-Star Games. Clemens's victory may have helped the American League turn things around. After the NL bounced back to win in 1987, the AL would go on to win the next six Midsummer Classics.

Carter was in his second season with the New York Mets in 1986. He hit a career-high 32 homers and drove in 100 runs in his first season in New York, finishing sixth in MVP voting as the Mets fought with the St. Louis Cardinals for the NL East title. He wasn't having as good an all-around year in '86, but his 16 home runs for the first-place Mets in the first half was enough to get him the starting nod. That meant just one at bat against Clemens.

He led off the second inning after Clemens mowed through the top three the NL had to offer in the first (that would be Tony Gwynn, Ryne Sandberg, and Keith Hernandez). Carter became out number four with a fly ball to center field. Carter, never lacking confidence (for good reason, what with the Hall of Fame plaque, the 2,000 games caught, the three Gold Gloves, five Silver Slugger Awards, etc.), came away impressed, but not awed by Clemens.

"I didn't find it overwhelming. I had an idea," Carter said. "He had very good control. I think that the ball was a little bit away from me and that's why I flew out to center. I got a little pumped up for All-Star Games... I was MVP in 1981 and 1984 and it's because you get a little bit extra excited. I hit two home runs in '81 and another one in '84, so I was looking to hit the ball hard somewhere."

Whether he succeeded in that endeavor is almost beside the point, though Carter certainly wasn't thinking that at the time. But in retrospect, Carter realizes it at least gave him a little heads-up for October. "I don't remember if I hit it hard or it was a lazy fly ball. But I do know it carried on to the World Series where at least I knew a little bit of his release point," Carter said. "That was my biggest thing about facing pitchers for the first time, knowing their release point and what kind of movement they had on their ball: if they had a devastating curve or sharp breaking ball. I think Roger was more of a fastball-kind with a breaking ball and every now and then a changeup. He just improved through the years because he came up with the split-finger. He really became a pitcher as time went on. To have the success he's had at age forty-four, he learned how to pitch. Back then, he may have been a little bit more of a thrower."

He was still "a thrower" come October. Of course he was a twenty-four-year-old who had finished off a magical season in which he went 24–4 with a league-leading 2.48 ERA. The season would earn him both the Cy Young and MVP Awards. He had gotten his postseason feet wet in the American League Championship Series with three starts against the Angels. After getting ripped in Game 1, he came back and pitched into the ninth in Game 4 before Calvin Schiraldi lost the game in the eleventh inning (a scenario that repeated itself later on against the Mets). He showed what he was made of by coming back on three days rest for Game 7 and allowing just 1 run over seven innings against a stunned Angels team that had coughed up a 3-1 series lead to send the Red Sox to the World Series in New York.

Gooden, for his part, was overpowering in his first trip to the playoffs. He allowed just 2 earned runs over seventeen innings, though he didn't get a win in either of his National League Championship Series starts. Gooden would actually appear in twelve postseason games over the course of his career and never come away with a victory.

The opening act to Clemens-Gooden Part II was a far less sexy Bruce Hurst–Ron Darling matchup in Game 1 of the World Series. As is often the case, it was the undercard that turned out to be better than the main event. Darling gave up 1 unearned run in seven innings, but Hurst was even stingier, going eight shutout frames to put the Sox up with a 1–0 win on the road. It also provided quite the changeup, going from the soft-tossing lefty to the fireballing young righty in Game 2. "That's an adjustment," Carter admitted. "That's usually how pitching staffs are set up. We had Bobby Ojeda mixed in between Doc Gooden and Ron Darling. Ojeda dazzled them with that changeup. Not an overpowering pitcher by any means, but [he] moved the ball back and forth quite well.

"You don't want to have two power pitchers in a row. You want to have a guy that's going to throw their timing off…That's how you mess them up, with their time. You have a guy like Bruce Hurst, who has that big over-the-top curveball. He had that high leg kick and good finish. He'd mix that changeup in and he'd bust that fastball inside and it would make his fastball that much faster. Yet he was not nearly as overpowering as a Roger Clemens."

Roger Clemens wasn't as overpowering as Roger Clemens could be in the much ballyhooed Game 2. Luckily for the Red Sox, Dwight Gooden wasn't really Dwight Gooden that night, either. Neither ace lasted past five innings, but it was Boston that walked away with a 9–3 victory and a commanding 2–0 lead as the Series headed to New England. "Doc Gooden compared to Roger Clemens. I really thought Gooden was the better of the two at that time," Carter said. "To have a matchup like that, it's like Randy Johnson versus Greg Maddux, or a Tom Seaver against a Bob Gibson, or a Sandy Koufax against a Juan Marichal. That's the kind of matchup we were looking at. That wasn't the way that game played out. Gooden didn't have his good stuff and he was pretty beat up in Game 2."

Gooden only went five innings, allowing 8 hits and 5 earned runs. Clemens didn't make it that far. He had a 6–2 lead heading into the fifth. He got the first out of the inning before walking Wally Backman for the second time, Clemens's fourth free pass of the game. After he allowed a Keith Hernandez single, he was lifted for reliever Steve Crawford with none other than Carter ready to dig in. "I was [surprised he was taken out]," Carter said. "To face a guy like Steve Crawford, [manager] John McNamara was doing me a favor. There must have been something bothering Roger. He was in line to get the victory and they pulled him before the end of the fifth inning."

Carter delivered an RBI single against Crawford to bring the Mets to within three runs, but the Red Sox bullpen shut the door after that while Boston's offense added three more runs. The Mets catcher hadn't been able to do much against even a struggling Clemens, flying out to center in the first and grounding out to end the third with a runner in scoring position, after the Mets had just put two runs on the board to close to within one run.

"Roger, you know he was going to challenge you, he was going to come at you," Carter said. "He had that good, live fastball. It's a matter of an adjustment of which way is he going to pitch me, is he going to go away, is he going to pitch me in? How is he going to come at me? That's the way you approach a guy like Roger Clemens, especially when you're facing him for the first, second, or third time.

"It's a matter that, you see on the on-deck circle, how he's approaching someone else and that's how you make that adjustment when you're at the plate. That's what I would do. Whoever was in the lineup that was comparable to my way of hitting was how I would make the adjustment. I would look at a particular hitter and follow the pattern of how he would throw to that particular hitter and that would pretty much be the way he would try to throw to me."

Carter would get another three chances against Clemens in Game 6, though everything that ultimately transpired in that classic game overshadowed who happened to start the game for the Red Sox. The Red Sox came back to Boston with a commanding 2–0 lead and Red Sox Nation thinking 1986 would be the year the championship drought would finally end after sixty-eight years. The Mets bounced back quickly, winning Games 3 and 4 behind strong pitching performances by Bobby Ojeda and Ron Darling. Bruce Hurst restored some faith in Beantown, beating Dwight Gooden with a complete-game performance in Game 5. That gave Hurst seventeen innings of World Series pitching and only two runs allowed, and set the stage for Game 6 back in New York.

The Sox took an early 2–0 lead against Ojeda on a Dwight Evans RBI double in the first and a Marty Barrett run-scoring single in the second. Not exactly an insurmountable lead, especially against a team that had won 108 games during the regular season that year, but the Sox faithful had to be feeling pretty good as Clemens put up zero after zero. The Mets didn't even pick up their first hit until the fifth inning, with only a Darryl Strawberry walk in the second inning keeping the Red Sox ace from being perfect. Carter contributed a second-inning fly out and fourth-inning ground out to the cause.

The Mets finally got something going in the fifth and got a little help from the Red Sox defense. Strawberry drew another walk to lead off the inning and stole second. Ray Knight's single drew the Mets to within a run. Knight was able to go to third on Mookie Wilson's single thanks to an error by Dwight Evans in right field. It turned out to be crucial since Knight was able to score when pinch hitter Danny Heep hit into a double play, knotting the score at 2–2 with an unearned run. New York had another chance against Clemens in the sixth. One-out singles by Wally Backman and Keith Hernandez put runners at the corners with the meat of the order up. But Carter, the cleanup hitter, was caught looking—Clemens's eighth and final strikeout of the game—and Strawberry grounded into a force play to end the threat. It was the only time Clemens did manage to strike out Carter, but it came at the most opportune time and kept the tie intact.

When the Red Sox untied it with their own unearned run in the top of the seventh, thanks to a Knight throwing error, and when Clemens had a 1-2-3 bottom of the inning, Red Sox fans dared hope that the time had finally come. And that's when things started getting weird, the kind of weird that forced even those least prone to believe in curses to dredge up the sale of Babe Ruth to the Yankees so many years earlier.

When Game 6 of this World Series is brought up, more often than not the first topic is Mookie Wilson's ground ball through Bill Buckner's legs, and for good reason. It was, after all, the game-winner. But the chain of events that fall evening began when Clemens, who had completed ten games during the season and appeared to be in complete command, was lifted for a pinch hitter in the top of the eighth inning. Granted, the Red Sox had a runner in scoring position with one out, but Clemens's removal has been a topic of some debate over time. Maybe it hasn't reached, "Why did John McNamara leave Buckner in to play first?" proportions, but there are plenty of second-guessers out there wondering exactly what happened.

McNamara maintained later that Clemens asked out of the game following the seventh because of a blister problem. He claims Clemens said, "That's all I can pitch." Clemens denies this and says he was yanked. To this day no one knows the real truth behind his removal. Instead, Schiraldi came in to pitch the eighth and allowed the tying run on a Carter sacrifice fly, with the Mets catcher getting the hit sign on a 3–0 count. Any Sox fan worth his or her salt can tell you the rest: Dave Henderson's tenth-inning homer nearly sent the city into seizure. The two-out collapse in the bottom of the inning, ending with Wilson's bounder through Buckner's wickets, sent it into catatonic shock and became the image most people associated with the Red Sox curse until they won the title in 2004. It led to Game 7, another meltdown by Schiraldi, and Bostonians everywhere looking for the nearest bridge.

Clemens's mysterious departure in Game 6 certainly gave Clemens an "incomplete" on his postseason report card. He finished with a 3.97 ERA in five playoff starts and he picked up just the one win, albeit in Game 7 of the ALCS. It continued in two future postseason performances with the Sox. He was never terrible, but he was rarely as overpowering as he was in the regular season. With some "help" from its bullpen, Boston went just 2–6 in Clemens's eight postseason starts between 1986 and 1990. He was able to reverse that somewhat with the Yankees, but perhaps it's the reason why Carter, while having respect for Clemens's abilities, never was wowed by him, even though he went hitless against him in seven at bats, including one final one in the 1988 All-Star Game. "I was impressed, but he wasn't a guy who, at that time, I would look at and say he was more overpowering than any of the great pitchers I had faced," Carter said.

It's difficult to say for sure if this is Carter's renowned self-confidence talking or something else. A player like Carter is never going to be in awe of anyone, but why didn't he walk away a little more amazed, especially considering he never managed to get a hit off Clemens? Maybe it was the fact that overall, Clemens wasn't as impressive in the World Series as he was during the season. Perhaps another hitter who saw Clemens only in postseason play, particularly in those early years, would have come away with the same reaction. Or maybe it's just the company Carter kept.

"One of them in particular, Tom Seaver," Carter said of some of the elite pitchers he faced over the course of his career. "When I first [established myself] in 1975, he was in the prime of his career. I came up at the end of 1974 and my second big-league hit was off of Tom Seaver. Once you establish that, you get hits off the best pitchers—my first home run was off Steve Carlton—you start believing you belong."

He particularly belonged against Carlton, the lefty Hall of Famer. Carter piled up 110 at bats against Carlton and picked up 34 hits for a .309 average. Eleven of those 34 hits were home runs—the most he hit against any pitcher—for an astounding .682 slugging percentage. He went just 12 for 64 (.188) with one homer against Seaver. He also faced Bob Gibson and stood in against Nolan Ryan forty-nine times.

"Here I was facing Roger Clemens in 1986 after my twelfth season in the big leagues," Carter said. "I was impressed, but I don't remember it being, 'Whoa, this guy is unbelievable. This guy is going to go on and win seven Cy Youngs and have the kind of career where he's looked at arguably as one of the best, if not the best, right-handers in the history of the game.'"

Of course Clemens evolved over the course of his career. Carter might have a hard time recognizing the pitcher who won Cy Young Awards with Toronto, New York, and Houston. "Back then, he was more of a thrower," Carter said. "As time went on, the success he was having, he learned how to pitch, how to move the ball in and out, which pitches to throw in certain situations. He just got better with age. He was a guru when it came to working out and that had a lot to do with his success, his work regimen."

Carter is the first to admit that he's dealing with an extremely small sample size. Yes, he faced Roger Clemens on the largest stages, but seven at bats are certainly not enough to draw a fair conclusion. Yet that's what makes baseball the game that it is, debating things like who the greatest right-hander of any generation is and the opinion of someone who took his hacks against a great number of them certainly carries some added weight.

"I didn't face Roger enough, as I did with Seaver," Carter admitted. "I got my share of hits off of Seaver. As far as knowing we were going to have to face him, you knew you really had to grind to even get a hit. I finally took him deep when he went to Cincinnati. Other than that, I never felt I would have a big day against a guy like that. I did better against a guy like Greg Maddux, more of a finesse pitcher. I have more lifetime home runs against Steve Carlton than any other pitcher, but he was left-handed. When Nolan Ryan came into the league, you knew how devastating a fastball he had, but he was a guy who would throw his breaking ball when he was behind in the count."

And yet, with all of those current and future Hall of Fame opponents, conversation invariably turns back to the guy who took the ball opposite Clemens both in that '86 All-Star Game and Game 2 of the Series: Doc

Gooden. Carter, to this day, will put up Gooden, circa 1985—his Cy Young Award year—against any pitcher in any league. "I'm always asked who was the best pitcher you ever caught and I say, no question, in that one season, in 1985, Doc Gooden was 24–4 with a 1.53 ERA and had 268 strikeouts," Carter said. "To me, he was the most devastating pitcher. He made hitters look foolish. And he was a two-pitch pitcher, fastball-curveball. They used to call a curveball an Uncle Charlie. His was a Lord Charles.

"I didn't see that in the at bats I faced Roger Clemens, that he was that devastating with one pitch. Doc Gooden had that good live fastball, but then he had that big curveball that would buckle guys' knees. I don't think that Roger at that time had one of those knee-bucklers. When you face a pitcher—Bert Blyleven, Barry Zito had/have that knee-buckler. Steve Carlton had that nasty slider. Bruce Sutter had that split-finger. Seaver had the fastball and a nasty slider. But all I know is that [Gooden] was the best pitcher I ever caught in my career, for that one year."

KEN GRIFFEY JR.

WHEN THE SUBJECT OF ROGER CLEMENS is broached with Ken Griffey Jr., he quickly boasts, "I own him!"

Then he pauses to consider his brash statement for a minute. Clemens is the ultimate competitor, after all, and the last thing Griffey needs is to give Clemens some bulletin board fodder if they should ever face each other again.

"What am I hitting against him?"

The numbers do support his claim. Over the years Junior Griffey has amassed 90 career at bats against Roger Clemens and has collected 28 hits along the way. That's a career .311 batting average for those of you scoring at home. Of those 28 base hits, 7 have been doubles and 6 have been home runs, giving him an outstanding .589 slugging percentage. Picking up 17 walks (one more than the 16 times he's struck out) leads to a .392 on-base percentage. He's second only to Jim Thome (8) in homers against the Rocket and he's fourth on the Clemens list with 16 RBIs. Only David Wells has given up more home runs to Griffey than Clemens has.

"See, I own him," Griffey Jr. said, breaking into a smile. "Nah, it's just one of those things. He's a pitcher who comes after you. He's going to give you a good pitch to hit and you have to be ready. He's not going to back down from a challenge. You have to be ready for it." And he was ready for it more often than not, though it took him a little while to get going at the outset of his career in the American League, and he didn't fare as well when both moved over to the National League. In between he's roughed up Roger Clemens about as much as any hitter ever has.

When the Boston Red Sox visited Seattle in 1989 and Roger Clemens took the mound on May 12, Ken Griffey Jr. was a whopping ninety-nine at bats into his big-league career. Not that people wondered who he was. The son of a former All-Star, the first overall pick of the 1987 draft, Griffey's ascension to big-league superstardom was always a matter of when and not if. Though he was just nineteen years old when he made the Mariners roster—Seattle had finished in last place with ninety-three losses in 1988 and had nothing to lose—he was already showing some impressive glimpses of what was to come from the future sure-to-be Hall of Fame center fielder.

Griffey was hitting .303 at the time of the Red Sox visit, though he had sat out for a couple of days following the team's 10–1 loss at Toronto on May 8. The M's, perhaps caught up in Junior fever, were a game over .500 at the time of the Boston series. By contrast, in the previous season Seattle was last above .500 on April 12.

The Red Sox were coming off a 1988 season that saw them barely win the AL East, by one game over the Tigers, with eighty-nine wins. When the Sox came to town for this three-game set, they were once again atop their division, with a slim half-game lead over the Yankees, and a game cushion over the Indians.

It was Clemens who got the ball in the series opener. He was twenty-six and had two Cy Young Awards, an MVP Award and two All-Star Game appearances under his belt. He had piled up seventy-eight wins heading into the season, and was 4–1 when he took the mound in the Kingdome. Clemens always liked pitching in the big domed stadium. What pitcher didn't? In seventeen starts there, he'd go 11–5 with a 2.71 ERA. This May start—the first one when he faced the teenaged Griffey Jr.—would be no different.

Clemens pitched a complete-game shutout that Friday night, allowing 2 hits, walking 1 and striking out 6. Griffey went 0 for 3 with a strikeout in his debut against the Rocket. He'd finish the year with a .264 average, 16 homers and 16 steals, enough to place third in AL Rookie of the Year voting. He may have had success against other pitchers, but the collar he took against Clemens wasn't the only one he got early on against the right-hander. The two would meet again almost exactly a year later with very similar results. Clemens went the distance, allowing 4 hits and just 1 run. Griffey went 0 for 2 with a walk. It wasn't like this was a case of a youngster not able to compete against his idol, someone he dreamt about as a teenager, but he does admit now that he was a bit awestruck in the early going.

"I didn't worry about Roger Clemens in high school," said Griffey, whose carefree on-field demeanor has always masked the true competitiveness within. "I was more or less being a typical teenage boy. It was girls and cars.

"But as a young hitter, you have a little bit of the, 'That's Nolan Ryan' or 'That's Roger Clemens.' Oh my, big named pitchers. You're in awe for a second because you're facing this guy. After that, you realize he's a pitcher and that's all he is. You can't say that to a nineteen- or twenty-year-old. You're watching him on TV, then you're going through the meetings and they're saying, 'This guy has done this, he's got this, he throws this, and he's like Cy Young.' Every pitcher you face at nineteen or twenty that has some credentials, he's like Cy Young. You're a little intimidated. After a couple of at bats, I was like, 'You can hit. Go out and hit.'"

He did just that in 1991. Clemens took the hill against the Mariners on June 19, in Fenway Park. Boston was in a tie for first place with the Toronto Blue Jays, the eventual AL East champions. Seattle was four games over .500, clearly headed in the right direction. The M's were in fifth place, but just four games out. They'd finish 83–79, the first time in franchise history they ended with a winning record. Perhaps the game against Clemens was a kind of microcosm for the season. In the previous two matchups during the early stages of the Junior Griffey era, Clemens had given up just a single run in eighteen innings. Seattle actually won this contest, touching the Boston ace for 9 hits and 4 runs (albeit just 1 of which was earned).

Griffey didn't waste much time breaking his schneid with an infield single in the first inning. He singled again in the third, but it was in the fifth that he really made his presence felt. With the Mariners trailing 2–1, Griffey doubled to right to knock in a pair of runs for his first extra-base hit and RBIs against the Rocket. For the day Griffey went 3 for 3 plus a walk against Clemens, as his Mariners held on to win, 4–3.

While their two other meetings in 1991 went more or less according to earlier form—Clemens had a complete-game win at the end of August and went nine innings in an extra-inning victory for the Red Sox just one start later—Junior's problems at the plate against Clemens were clearly a thing of the past. He went 1 for 3 with a double in that August game and then went 2 for 4 with a pair of RBIs and another two-base hit in their last contest of the year. It was the first of three straight 100-RBI seasons for Griffey. He also made the second of eleven consecutive All-Star appearances.

Before anyone thinks Griffey only had gap power against Clemens, the first long ball came the following year, in 1992. While he extended his Clemens hit streak to four games in their first meeting, he went yard in their second encounter, in Seattle. Clemens was masterful at the Kingdome yet again, going eight innings and yielding just a single run. That run came in the fourth when Griffey led off the frame with a home run. To some, hitting one out against a pitcher of Clemens's caliber would indeed be something special. Griffey, though, tries to downplay the occasion. "At that time it was my fourth year. I'd seen him before. It really wasn't that big of a deal," Griffey said. "The biggest thing was to not embarrass him or yourself, because he has the ball. You just go out there. He can be beatable. He has some losses."

The Mariners handed one to him later on in 1992, tagging Clemens for 6 runs over six innings. Although Griffey didn't get a hit off of Clemens—he would triple off reliever Paul Quantrill—he did walk twice and score twice. Clemens won the fourth and final meeting between the two teams with another complete-game performance in September. With a 2-for-4 (including a double) showing, Griffey went a combined 11 for 23 from 1991 to 1992 after beginning his career 0 for 5 against Clemens. Five of those 11 hits were of the extra-base variety—4 doubles and the home run—and he drove in 5 runs. Perhaps even more impressive is that he drew 4 walks and struck out only twice in that span. "I was just young, feeling out guys," Griffey said. "I was trying to pick up tendencies that he had and went from there. He threw hard and you just had to be ready."

That, of course, meant ready for anything, including an upper-90s fastball up under your chin. Clemens has always used his ability to pitch inside to make hitters less than comfortable at the plate. His aura and mound presence have always been effective against hitters just coming into the league. Sometimes just being Roger Clemens was enough to keep a young hitter from really being able to dig in at the plate. But that tactic never really worked against Griffey. Growing up around the game, watching his father play for years, being brushed back usually elicited a ho-hum kind of response from Junior.

Clemens could try to knock Griffey down, but that wouldn't keep him from getting his hacks in.

"That's toward younger hitters, not so much to the guys who have been around, the intimidation factor, I'm going to throw one up and in," Griffey said. "Me being a son of a former baseball player—at the time a baseball player—you could throw one up and in and I'd forget about it. That's not what I cared about. It didn't bother me. He still has to throw it across the plate and you still have a chance to hit it."

He continued taking advantage of those chances in 1993. His first at bat against Clemens, in late April, produced an RBI single, though that would be the lone hit in six plate appearances versus the Rocket. While Griffey had been productive in his previous four seasons, 1993 proved to be a breakout of sorts, particularly in the power department. It was his first 40-home-run season, as his 45 placed him second only to Juan Gonzalez in the league. He topped the junior circuit in total bases and extra-base hits, while finishing second in slugging and third in OPS (on-base plus slugging). It was a tough year for Clemens as he battled first a groin injury and then an elbow problem en route to finishing the season with an 11–14 record and un-Clemens like 4.46 ERA.

If '93 was a breakout, then 1994 was when Griffey put himself into the stratosphere. He had another 40-homer season, which doesn't sound that impressive until one remembers that this was the strike-shortened season. Junior's 40 homers that year came in 150 fewer at bats than he had in 1993. He won his first home run title while finishing third in slugging, OPS, and extra-base hits. The only thing that kept him from winning MVP honors was the monstrous season Frank Thomas had at the same time.

His big season translated into more success against Clemens as well. Griffey took the Rocket deep for the second time in their first matchup of the season, a solo shot in a terrific Roger Clemens versus Randy Johnson battle. The Big Unit won that one, 4–2, though Clemens gave up just one earned run—Junior's long ball—in the loss. Griffey collected two more hits near the end of the abbreviated season to bring his career average against Clemens up to .459 (17 for 37). This wasn't a case of Griffey taking advantage of a subpar Rocket. Clemens returned to form in 1994, finishing second in the American League in ERA and strikeouts.

If Clemens couldn't get him out, the Red Sox did have someone who could. Lefty reliever Tony Fossas came in on two separate occasions after Clemens to strike out Griffey during the 1994 season. One explanation might merely be the change of pace, going from a fireballing right-hander to a lefty who could barely break a pane of glass. Griffey disagrees, claiming it was simply because Fossas had his number throughout his career. The numbers concur with the center fielder: Griffey went just 3 for 24 against Fossas.

"Tony Fossas is not a good example," Griffey said of the "changeup" theory. "I couldn't hit him anyway. You have a drop-down lefty who throws from the first base side and doesn't throw very hard. He keeps throwing the curveball further and further away. At that time I kept swinging and swinging and swinging. I couldn't hit him. Now, I just don't swing at them."

The 1995 season was not a good one for Griffey personally, though it turned out to be an outstanding one for the Mariners. The season didn't get underway until the end of April and Griffey's year was nearly over by the end of May. He shattered his wrist on May 26 making a catch in right-center field in the Kingdome and missed nearly three months of the season. He did return by the middle of August and his big September helped the Mariners make the playoffs for the first time in franchise history as the AL West Division champions. They went on to beat the New York Yankees in five games in the American League Division Series as part of the first postseason of the wild card era. It was Griffey who came around to score from first base on an Edgar Martinez's double in the eleventh inning to send the Yankees home. Griffey hit .391 with 5 home runs in that series, then hit .333 in the ALCS, though the Mariners lost to the Cleveland Indians in six games.

While everyone's season started late in 1995 because of the strike, Clemens was even tardier. He made his first start of the season on June 2, at Fenway Park against the Seattle Mariners, after beginning the season on the disabled list with a strained muscle behind his right shoulder. Like the M's that year, the Red Sox won their division, but then lost to the Indians in the ALDS. Clemens would go 10–5 on the year, but his 4.18 ERA may have signaled the beginning of the end of his tenure in Boston. He allowed 5 runs over five innings against the Mariners that day, a game the Red Sox eventually won in ten innings. Griffey, out with his broken wrist, wasn't able to continue his hot streak against the Rocket.

The 1996 season turned out to be Clemens's last with the Red Sox and while his 3.63 ERA and 257 strikeouts were among the league leaders—he actually topped the American League in K's—there was an unpleasant divorce between pitcher and team and Clemens went on to sign with the Blue Jays the following season. Griffey had a monster season in '96, hitting 49 homers in the first of five straight 40-homer seasons for the center fielder. His 140 RBIs were a career high, and he finished fourth in the league's MVP vote behind Juan Gonzalez, teammate Alex Rodriguez, and Albert Belle. He was better against the rest of the league than he was against Clemens that year. He did hit his third homer off the legend in their first meeting, but he went a combined 2 for 10 on the year versus the Red Sox starter. That put his career numbers at 19 for 47, still a robust .404 average.

Clemens then moved on to Toronto where he experienced what most people consider a rebirth of sorts on the mound. The biggest reason, of course, was the addition of the split-fingered fastball to his repertoire, giving him another nasty out pitch. Griffey, though, thinks it may have been more than just expanding his pitch choices. With his tenure ending in Boston acrimoniously, maybe it was simply putting on a new uniform that returned Clemens to elite status.

"Sometimes, you just need a change of scenery to recharge the batteries," Griffey offered. "It's worked.

It worked in Houston, too. Sometimes you need that. Boston, I guess for him, at the time, was a little rough on him. He felt a change was needed and he decided to go out and win Cy Young again. Twice."

When Clemens and Griffey did battle in 1997, it would be hard to find anyone who would dispute that it was a marquee matchup between the best pitcher and best hitter in the American League that season. While Clemens was winning his fifth Cy Young Award, Griffey was capturing his one, and only, MVP honor. He did so by leading the league in a host of offensive categories, including home runs (56), RBIs (147), slugging percentage (.646), runs scored (125), total bases (393), and extra-base hits (93).

He also returned to battering Clemens, starting with their first meeting in late April at Skydome in Toronto. The Canadian park has always been one of Griffey's favorite to hit in, with a career .305 average and .593 slugging percentage in forty-four games. The 14 home runs he's hit there is his fourth-highest total at an away stadium. He hit 3 on April 25, 1997, 2 against Clemens and another against reliever Mike Timlin. All were solo shots, as the Mariners beat the Blue Jays, 13–8, though Clemens got a no-decision in the game. "I hit one to right field, then came up a couple of at bats later and hit one to left," Griffey recalled. "He [Clemens] said, 'You can't have both sides of the plate. You better choose one.' I said, 'I chose the left and then chose the right at the right time. If you had thrown it down the middle, I wouldn't have swung.'"

The home run Griffey hit in that game off Timlin would give him 13 for the month of April. He hit the

All-Star break with 30 home runs. The following sea-son—the one made famous by Mark McGwire and Sammy Sosa in the National League—he had 35 at the break, 2 more than Sosa and just 2 fewer than Big Mac. He went on a huge power surge at the end of the 1997 season, hitting 12 homers in August and an-other dozen in September to inch close to what was then the single-season home run record of 61. When he faced Clemens in Seattle on September 12, he was at 50. He had picked up a double off the Rocket, good for 2 RBIs, back in June and he would again be held homerless for a second time, going 1 for 4 with a strikeout in the September game. Three days later, in the series finale with the Jays, he hit a couple out against Woody Williams, but he'd finish the season five home runs shy of the mark.

In 1998 Griffey had 47 homers entering the final month of the season. One came off Clemens, again in Toronto. The May 18 blast was a three-run shot in the fourth inning and helped chase the Cy Young winner after five innings. It was Junior's 16th home run of the season. Clemens would get some measure of revenge in August as he tossed a three-hit shutout and hung an 0 for 4 on Griffey. The Mariners center fielder would again finish five home runs shy of Roger Maris's record while McGwire and Sosa were shattering it in the senior circuit.

Griffey was no stranger to the home-run talk. He long was considered the favorite—based on his num-bers and his age—to eventually catch Hank Aaron and his 755 career homers. Even though he crept close to the single-season mark a couple of times and was close to a record-setting pace in 1994 as well, his name never came up all that much in discussions of Maris's record. That was fine by Griffey, who doesn't care to discuss records or statistics. "I don't even think about those things," Griffey said. "Those aren't things you worry about. I have to worry about the guy standing sixty feet from me, not some record. That's the most important thing ... the guy I'm looking at. Not the records you guys look at. I don't worry about the records. Some people have that for motivation. My motivation is to go out there and be the best baseball player I can be. And that's it."

As the 1990s started to wind down, it would have been hard to argue with a characterization of Griffey as the best baseball player in the league and perhaps in all of baseball. Sure, there were many Barry Bonds supporters and those who would back the younger Mariner Alex Rodriguez. But Griffey was at or near the top of everyone's list of best players of the decade. He did nothing to detract from that in 1999, hitting 48 homers and driving in 134 runs for another top 10 MVP finish.

Clemens, meanwhile, had been dealt from the Blue Jays to the Yankees. He would go on to win his first World Series ring that season. The resumption of the Clemens versus Griffey battle would be a two-game showdown. Junior went 1 for 3 with an RBI single in early August, as Clemens beat the Mariners in Seattle, 7–4. At the end of the month, the M's came to New York and Clemens was much more stingy, going eight shutout innings, allowing just 4 hits while striking out 9. Griffey went 0 for 2 with a walk and a strikeout.

That would be the last meeting between the two players for four years. Griffey was traded to the Cincinnati Reds in the off-season and there were no Yankees-Reds interleague matchups over the next few years. At the close of the decade, and a ten-year American League battle, Griffey had gone a combined 27 for 74 against Clemens for a .365 average to go along with 6 career home runs against the right-hander.

While the concept of Ken Griffey Jr. having success against any pitcher in the 1990s should neither be shocking nor surprising, his "owning" of Roger Clemens during a decade that saw the pitcher win three Cy Young Awards does call for further inspection. What was Griffey's secret? How did he manage to light up the Rocket when the rest of the American League looked foolish more often than not?

Junior Griffey didn't have a much different approach when facing Clemens than he did while striking fear into the hearts of most of the league's pitchers. One of the keys to Clemens's dominance over the past two decades has been his ability to not let hitters get comfortable in the box. Griffey's hitting philosophy was very similar: don't let the pitcher settle in and find his rhythm.

"I was just trying to get him early," Griffey explained. "He's one of those pitchers as the game goes on, he zones in to how he pitches. If you get him early and get him out, you don't have to worry about him. But he's the kind of pitcher that gets stronger and stronger as the game goes on because he knows what you like and what you don't like and he has a feel for each hitter the second and third time around.

"The truth is, though, you want to get every pitcher early. If you get pitchers early, you get them out; you get in the bullpen. That's what you want."

Most people would file that under the "much easier said than done" category, but for a talent like Griffey, it really could be that simple. It also helped that he had family to lean on for help. Ken Griffey Sr. had a distinguished career, most notably as part of the Big Red Machine that won back-to-back titles in 1975–76. He ended his career as a teammate of his son's in Seattle in 1990 and 1991. Throughout his career Junior could count on Senior to give sage hitting advice. It didn't hurt that both hit left-handed and the younger had hitting mechanics that looked a lot like the elder's approach. "It's always an advantage when a guy you swing like has faced him. That's a big advantage," Griffey admitted.

It certainly helped as it pertained to batting against a guy like Clemens. Griffey Sr. didn't have the long history his son would have against the Rocket, but there was enough of a track record that he could speak with some authority. The elder Griffey went 5 for 9 against Clemens in his career. Coupling that with simple hitting know-how helped him aid his son in their approach against Clemens, even after Clemens developed that split-finger fastball so many credit with reviving his career in Toronto. "Over the years my dad just said, 'Don't swing at the splitter and you'll have a better at bat and you'll have a better chance of getting him,'"

Griffey Jr. said. "That's what you just lay off of. I knew that listening to my dad. That was the one thing he said, if you stay off of that, you're going to be fine."

Griffey understands that by no means was this a guarantee of success. Neither was hitting from the left side, though some might think it would be easier for a southpaw to pick up the splitter. He managed to recognize the pitch more often than not, and the advice from Dad helped him to remember that he should let it go by. "It's still tough," Griffey said. "Once he starts moving away and going down, you try to lay off because you know what it is. He's not going to try to throw the splitter into a lefty. He's going to leave it on the outside part of the plate. So don't worry about it."

They say that respect is a two-way street; that axiom is no truer than in the baseball world. While that avenue between hitter and pitcher definitely was established with Griffey's success against Clemens in the batter's box, there's more to it than that. Again, having a father with more than 2,000 games of big-league experience came in handy. Junior Griffey certainly more than established himself on his own merits, but he understands there was an immediate acceptance just because of the last name on his jersey. "I think it's a little bit different because my dad played," Griffey said. "There's always a little different respect factor when your dad played. They know him. They'd seen me at the ballpark. So it's a little different respect factor than for someone else he's never seen before. Having a name in baseball does help sometimes. Just sometimes."

Not that Griffey was willing to skate by on his name alone. Just a teenager when he came into the league, he found a way to forge a relationship with Clemens in another way, and not on the field. Fairly early on, he formed a bond through Clemens's kids, who were in some ways closer in generation to Griffey than their dad was. "It was a little different. I'm not that much older than his kids," Griffey said. "I had the same interests they did—Nintendo—at the time. You go after the kids first. Then you work on the dad. I kept telling them to have their dad throw it down the middle 85 miles per hour and I promise I'll hit it to left field. If he throws it a little harder, I'm going to try to hit it to right. That's how we became friends."

Friend is not a word tossed around loosely by opponents of Clemens. Clemens has always been known as an exemplary teammate, but his desire to keep the opposition at arm's length is almost legendary. He's never been one to let his guard down, even with league teammates at All-Star Games, for fear of giving up the edge he has used so masterfully for more than two decades on the mound. Yet Griffey found a way into that inner sanctum and their friendship grew over the years. Their relationship grew not just during the regular-season matchups, but the five times the two were American League All-Stars together in the 1990s.

After Griffey was traded to Cincinnati prior to the 2000 season, the relationship was put on hold for nearly five years. But they picked up where they left off prior to their first meeting at the end of April

2004, Clemens's fifth start in an Astros uniform. The friendship has never been based on baseball, so when they reunited, and in other instances when they met over the next few years, they would talk about life outside the game. It's something Griffey feels players share more than most people not in baseball understand.

"'How're the boys doing?' He started explaining," Griffey recalled the conversation.

"'Are they playing football?' He said, 'Yeah. Koby and Kody [are] playing baseball now.' The first thing is always, no matter what, at the time, 'How's your mom doing?' He broke it down. Even last year in the WBC, got to talking, he was explaining some things about the last couple of months with his mom, and how she was.

"That's what guys really care about. You could be struggling and we don't care. But we do care about everyone's families and their well-being. That's the most important thing. Baseball can only last so long, but your family, your friends, are there forever."

Griffey's success against Clemens wasn't as everlasting as that common bond. As dominant as he had been in the decade prior, he was that ineffective when both were in the National League Central from 2004 to 2006. It started with that first meeting in April 2004, when Junior went 0 for 2 with a walk against Clemens, who allowed just a single run over six innings to run his record to a perfect 5–0. This pushed the Astros into a first-place tie with the Cubs, two games ahead of the Reds. A month later, the Reds roughed the Rocket up a bit, tagging him for 9 hits and 6 runs over five innings, though Clemens didn't figure into the decision. It turned out to be a Reds victory, but Griffey didn't contribute offensively until Clemens was out of the game. He was 0 for 3 with 2 strikeouts against the Rocket, and then hit an RBI double against Astros closer Brad Lidge. The win moved the Reds into a three-way tie atop the division with the Astros and Cubs.

It was the first time that the two future Hall of Famers were in the same division and that a win or loss against each other would have such a direct impact on the standings. Griffey remained pragmatic about it and downplayed the significance of Clemens coming to the NL Central. "He's not on my team," Griffey said bluntly. "He can only pitch once a week, maybe twice a week. Hopefully, the team he's facing is hot."

By the time the two teams met again in September, the Astros were hot, at least from a wild card perspective, but the Reds were not. The St. Louis Cardinals had run away and hid, holding a 17½ game lead over the Cubs, 18 games over the Astros. The Reds, who started out so promisingly, had faded and were in fourth place, 29½ games out of first. The Cubs and Astros, though, were at the top of the National League wild card standings, so every game in September was crucial for Houston. Clemens went seven strong innings in the final game against Cincinnati, allowing just a single run and improving to 16–4 en route to Cy Young Award number seven. The Astros would go on to win the wild card before losing to the Cardinals in the National League Championship Series.

For the second time in his career, Griffey was not able to take the field when Clemens took the mound. It had been an eventful season for Junior in the first half. He hit career home run number 500 in June, on Father's Day with Senior in attendance. Coincidentally, he also picked up hit number 2,143 to tie him with his father. But then he injured his hamstring in early July, keeping him from attending his twelfth All-Star Game. He came back just shy of a month later but managed just five at bats over three games before he completely ruptured his hamstring, ending his season. His absence undoubtedly contributed to the Reds swoon in the second half of the year.

After managing to play in just eighty-three games in 2004 (after seventy in 2002 and just fifty-three in 2003), Griffey was relatively healthy in 2005. He collected 491 at bats over 128 games, hitting 35 homers, driving in 92 runs, and hitting .301. He couldn't escape the injury bug entirely, though, playing his last game of the year in early September due to a strained tendon in his left foot. His 35 home runs did put him in a tie with Mickey Mantle on the career homer list.

None of those long balls came against Clemens as Junior's struggles against the Rocket continued, beginning with Clemens's first start of the 2005 season. Playing in Houston, Clemens struck out 9 over seven innings, including Griffey twice. The Reds actually beat Clemens in Houston at the end of May, though the right-hander was sharp. Griffey, however, wore another collar, going 0 for 3 against the Astros starter. He finally broke the "0 for" on July 3 with a 1 for 3 performance, though Clemens tossed seven shutout innings that Sunday afternoon. The Astros once again finished in distant second place to the Cardinals, but they won the wild card and went on to the World Series. The Reds, once again, finished in the second division, twenty-seven games behind St. Louis.

With the 2006 season came another Griffey injury. This time it was a knee problem that forced him to miss a month early in the year. A dislocated toe kept him out of action for three weeks in September. In between he squeezed in 109 games and 27 more home runs. The Reds and Astros closed quickly on a slumping Cardinals team, with both teams staying in the NL Central hunt well into September, but neither team had enough to overtake the eventual World Series champions.

Clemens and Griffey didn't meet up until late July 2006, largely because of Clemens's delayed decision to rejoin the Astros. He didn't make his first start until June 22 and when he took the mound against Cincinnati on July 25, it was just his seventh start of the season. Aaron Harang outdueled Clemens that night, winning 2–0, but the Astros right-hander again had Griffey's number, keeping the left-handed slugger hitless in three at bats. For the record, that made Griffey 1 for 14 against Clemens in the NL.

When Clemens pitched against the Reds for the final time, on September 20, the Reds were 1½ games ahead of the Astros in second place in the NL Central, 4½ games out of the wild-card lead. Clemens beat the Reds with six shutout innings, with Griffey out of the lineup with his injured toe. It wasn't an easy thing for Griffey to deal with.

"It's tough. Any time you have to sit and watch somebody else play, it's tough," Griffey said. "You want your team to do well. It's tough when one of your top guys is out, whether it's me, Adam Dunn, Austin Kearns at the time. It just makes it tough when one of your big dogs is not in the lineup because of injuries late in the year."

It's something Griffey jokes he and Clemens have shared the last year or so, watching their respective teams play from the sidelines. Of course, quips Griffey, he was forced to the sidelines while Clemens's time as a spectator has been voluntary. "Mine was because of injuries," he laughed. "He gets to sit home until May because he wants to. Tell him I'm coming back as a pitcher. And I only want to pitch road games. That's my new gig, my new contract."

Not everyone can take a swipe, however playful, at Clemens like that and it speaks volumes about their relationship. He's seen a side of Clemens few have and even claims to have seen the Rocket's lighter side on the mound. "He's got a good sense of humor," Griffey said. "A couple of times he threw ones way up and in, I hooked it foul. He threw another one closer and he yelled at me, 'Hit that one!' So then I singled to left."

As much fun as they might have from time to time on the field and as close a bond as they have forged away from it through their families, there's never been any doubt about what the main objective is when Clemens is on the mound and Griffey is in the box. Perhaps they can share the rare joke and confide in each other when they have the opportunity, but it's all business when it comes to the competition. When it's Griffey versus Clemens, there's never any let up from either side of the equation.

"Once he's on the mound, he's still going to be a totally different animal," Griffey said. "He's not going to give in; he's going to try and beat you. He's going to come with his best and I'm going to come with my best. May the best man win on that at bat. If he gets me, I have to come back stronger the next at bat. If I get him, I know he's going to come back and dig a little deeper to get me out."

It's that competitive fire, that inner desire to best an opponent, that undoubtedly has helped Griffey come back from countless serious injuries. And there's no question it's what keeps Clemens coming back year after year, even belatedly. Just how long he can keep it going, no one is sure. Not even a friend like Griffey. Perhaps Clemens will keep on going until he reaches the half-century mark, to prove a point that he could. Perhaps not. That's one thing Griffey is sure won't happen.

"I don't think [Roger's wife] Debbie is going to allow that," Griffey said with a smile. "One day, she's going to put her foot down and say, 'Come home.'"

WORLD SERIES
OPPONENTS

CHIPPER **JONES** (1999)

CHIPPER JONES AND ROGER CLEMENS have had their most memorable meetings in high-pressure situations, like the final game of a World Series and in extra innings of one of the most exciting National League Division Series games in history. Who would have thought that their very first on-field meeting came in Rhode Island?

On July 12, 1993, Chipper Jones was playing shortstop for the Richmond Braves, Atlanta's Triple-A affiliate. He was an International League All-Star who would finish the year hitting .325 with 13 homers and 89 RBIs before making his big-league debut that September. His teammates in Richmond that year included catcher Javy Lopez and first baseman/outfielder Ryan Klesko. (All three would contribute to the 1995 World Series–winning team and helped the Braves keep their string of division titles going for many years.)

Back in 1993, however, they were still gazing up at the big leagues, though Klesko and Lopez had gotten tastes of the majors. Jones, the first player taken in the 1990 baseball draft, was still waiting for his first call up when Richmond traveled to Pawtucket to face the

Red Sox Triple-A affiliate. On the mound July 12 was a rehabbing big-league starter coming back from a groin injury. It was Roger Clemens's first and only appearance with the PawSox and he didn't disappoint the capacity crowd at McCoy Stadium in Pawtucket.

Overall, the 1993 season was not a great one for Clemens. Of course he had set the bar pretty high, with the three Cy Young Awards and one MVP already on his resume. Because of the injury, though, Clemens's streak of 200-plus-inning seasons was snapped at seven. He also had his first losing season at 11–14 and his 4.46 ERA was more than two runs higher than his mark the previous year. While wins are often not in a pitcher's control, he did go a rather un-Clemens-like 40–39 over the next three seasons before his move to Toronto in 1997.

It would have been hard to prove to the Richmond Braves, who tried and failed against him that July night, that he wasn't the same Rocket. Over 3⅔ scoreless innings, he struck out 8, walked 4, and allowed just 1 hit. While his command was still a bit off, he did manage to strike out two batters in each inning. As is often the case when big-time major-league stars come back to the minors for rehab assignments (a scene repeated years later when Clemens went on his "return from retirement" tours), there's no doubt the Richmond club was duly impressed and in awe of Clemens's persona. Chipper Jones was just twenty-one at the time, but he stored away the information of what it was like to try to dig in against Clemens in case he would need it later in his career.

When Jones first arrived in the bigs that only could have happened in the World Series or an All-Star Game. While Clemens was finishing up his Red Sox career, Jones's own path became a bit crooked. Slated by the Braves to move to left field to get his bat into the everyday lineup in 1994—Terry Pendleton was the incumbent at third and Jeff Blauser manned shortstop—Jones tore his ACL in Spring Training and missed the entire season. He came back with a vengeance in 1995, finishing second in National League Rookie of the Year voting to Japanese import Hideo Nomo after hitting 23 homers and driving in 86 runs. He showed nerves of steel by hitting .364 over the course of the postseason, excelling particularly in the first-ever National League Division Series and in the National League Championship Series. Winning a World Series in your rookie season can be a mixed blessing. The expectations are easily set that winning the World Series is what you do every year. Yet Jones and the Braves took home just that one ring in 1995 during their run of divisional titles that began in 1991 and continued through 2005.

In 1996, Clemens's last with the Red Sox, the switch-hitting Jones made his first All-Star team and finished fourth in the league MVP vote, won by Ken Caminiti of the San Diego Padres. He finished the season with 110 RBIs, the first of eight consecutive seasons the Braves third baseman finished over the century mark in runs batted in. He had another solid postseason, hitting .346 overall. But he and the Braves faced the Cleveland Indians in the 1995 Fall

Classic and the Yankees in the '96 Series, so that first-hand Clemens knowledge didn't come in handy.

Then came the advent of interleague play in 1997. The Braves first taste of it was at home against the Baltimore Orioles. The Braves likely weren't huge fans right out of the gate, as the O's swept them in Atlanta. They went from there to Toronto where they would face the resurgent Clemens in the series opener. Clemens was 11–1 at the time and well on his way to Cy Young Award number four. Jones was hitting .290 with 8 homers and 48 RBIs and was bouncing back from a poor May by hitting .333 with 3 homers and 15 RBIs in the first fourteen games of June. He'd end up hitting 8 homers and driving in 29 runs for the whole month en route to another All-Star appearance.

Clemens went the distance in that game, striking out 12 while walking none. But he gave up 3 runs while Braves starter Denny Neagle tossed a five-hit shutout, so Clemens was a tough-luck loser and got saddled with just his second "L" of the season. Jones had a lot to do with it. Hitting in the cleanup spot, he singled to lead off the second inning and came around to score the first run of the game—the only one the Braves ended up needing—on a Klesko double.

The big blow came with one out in the sixth. Keith Lockhart had struck out to open the inning, then Jones took Clemens deep to give the Braves a 3–0 lead. It would be the only time in his career Jones homered off of Clemens and it's a memory he won't soon forget.

"I kind of had a feel as to what was in store for us," Jones said, thinking back to his 1993 matchup in

Pawtucket. "Anytime you're facing a guy like that, you're chomping at the bit to get up there. I remember rounding first base thinking, 'I just took the Rocket deep' and thinking how proud my parents would be of me. I think when you take a guy like him deep, you earn his respect. That's all you want as a ballplayer, to have the respect of your peers and the best players in the game, and I certainly think Roger has that."

Jones nearly lost that recently won respect in his next at bat. He led off the ninth inning and Clemens was still on the mound. This was the first year Clemens started using the split-fingered fastball and he threw one in the dirt. Then Jones made what was perhaps an unwise decision. "Charlie O'Brien, who was my teammate the year before, was catching," Jones recalled. "I asked the umpire to check the ball and Charlie kind of snaps his head up and says, 'You know who that is out there?' I said, 'Check the ball.' Next pitch . . . whoosh, chin music. It was the older veteran, the stud, showing the [young guy] what's going on."

Even though he lost that game, it was clear what was going on: Clemens was back as one of the best, if not *the* best, right-handers in the game. He had begun his first reinvention, with the split-fingered fastball as his primary tool. "I guess in Toronto he started to throw it," Jones said. "It was probably his third best pitch then. Now he'd probably tell you he gets the majority of his outs with that split-finger.

"I think he will tell you he was kind of in a lull— that's not the right word—his numbers weren't, for the previous couple of years, what we'd expect from Roger Clemens. But when he got that split and started learning how to throw it and use it, his career took off, again. Not only did he have the overpowering heater, he had the devastating split to put you away with, too."

He wouldn't have a chance to put away Jones or the Braves again for three years, when interleague play brought them together again in July 1999. Clemens was again in his first season with a new team, the New York Yankees, though that debut campaign did not go nearly as well as his first season north of the border. The Rocket went 14–10 in 1999, and had a 4.60 ERA, the only time in his career where he finished with an ERA higher than the league mark.

The Braves visited New York for a three-game set to open the second half of the season following the All-Star break. Anytime the Braves and Yankees met, it was a big deal. The foundation for a good interleague rivalry had been laid with the 1996 World Series. The opener of this series featured Clemens versus Tom Glavine, one of those marquee matchups fans really looked forward to, but Clemens gave up 6 runs on 6 hits and 5 walks over six innings to fall to 8-4 on the year. Jones went 1 for 3, walking twice and scoring twice.

"It takes a little adjusting, your first time in New York," said Jones, meaning it more as an explanation than an excuse for Clemens's up-and-down season. "It's a tough place to play. They were probably picked to win it, obviously with him coming in, it probably was a little adjustment for him and guys probably jumped on him a little bit."

Jones was jumping on everyone in 1999. Playing at age twenty-seven—that magical age when good players tend to have their best or breakout seasons— Jones won the National League MVP Award, getting all but one first-place vote to easily beat Jeff Bagwell. He also picked up the first of two straight Silver Slugger Awards after hitting a career high 45 home runs, driving in 110 runs, hitting .319 and stealing 25 bases to boot. It was the only season that Jones topped the 40-home-run plateau. Coming off of a huge second half, his confidence was sky-high as the Braves entered the postseason for the eighth straight year.

Clemens, meanwhile, had limped a bit getting to the finish line of the regular season. He went 2–4 with a 5.21 ERA in six September starts. But it was the then-thirty-six-year-old right-hander who would have the last laugh when the teams met for the second time in four years for the World Series title.

Clemens helped finish off the sweep of the Rangers in the American League Division Series with seven innings of three-hit shutout ball, but his ALCS start is one he'd rather forget. In a greatly hyped marquee matchup of Roger Clemens versus Pedro Martinez at Fenway, Clemens got chased after facing just one batter in the third inning, allowing 5 runs on 6 hits. Martinez put up zeroes for seven innings, yielding just 2 hits and 2 walks while striking out 12. It ended as a 13–1 laugher.

All of that would be forgotten eleven days later when Clemens took the mound with a chance to give the Yankees their third championship in four years in

Game 4 of the World Series. The Braves's best chance to make the Series competitive may have been in Game 1. In a pitcher's duel between Orlando Hernandez and Greg Maddux in Atlanta, the Braves clung to a 1–0 lead into the eighth inning. It was a Jones home run in the fourth inning that gave Atlanta the lead, one they felt would hold up with Maddux on the top of his game.

"Doggie [Maddux's nickname is Mad Dog] went back out and they scored four runs off of him in the eighth," said Jones about the eventual 4–1 Yankee victory. "It was a demoralizing loss, a game we felt we had in hand with Greg Maddux on the mound. You pretty much felt it was over. To the Yankees credit, they stuck with it, strung together some hits and really took the wind out of our sails. That was the first time in the Series they did it and they did it again in Game 3."

The Yankees won Game 2, 7–2, scoring five runs in the first three innings to take any mystery out of the game. The Series shifted to New York with the Yankees holding a 2–0 series lead. Then came Game 3. To the Braves credit they battled back and held a 5–2 lead heading into the seventh. The Yankees picked up a run on a Tino Martínez home run in the seventh, but the Braves once again felt good with Tom Glavine on the mound.

But much like with Maddux two games earlier, things unraveled in the eighth inning. Joe Girardi singled to lead off the inning and Chuck Knoblauch followed with a surprising two-run homer to tie the score and chase Glavine from the game. It remained tied until the bottom of the tenth inning when Chad Curtis, who had homered in the fifth inning off of Glavine, hit a walk-off homer to lead off the tenth and give the Yankees a commanding 3–0 series lead. The Braves knew that not only did they have to try to come back from that deficit—something that's never been done in World Series history—they'd have to start doing it against Roger Clemens in Game 4.

"It was a tall task," Jones admitted. "Game 3 really took it out of us. We had that game in hand and let it slip away from us late, so it was pretty demoralizing. We knew runs were going to be scarce [in Game 4]. Once they got the lead in that game, it was pretty much over. Our psyche was pretty bruised and he capitalized. He was pretty dominant that night."

It wasn't the same kind of dominance Jones saw from Clemens during that first interleague matchup or way back in that rehab start. Even though he had developed the splitter back in 1997, he still would rear back and throw the fastball by you when he wanted to. When it came to facing Jones in Game 4, he clearly remembered the home run the Brave third baseman hit in that interleague meeting.

There are hitters who can hit a fastball. Then there are those who can turn on a good heater. And then there's Chipper Jones. It's not a stretch to say that Jones is one of the best pure fastball hitters in the game. Period. There isn't a fastball he can't hit and hit hard. There are times when it's fine to go power versus power. Sometimes the closer with the triple-digit stuff will get one by a hitter like Jones, but Clemens realized that Game 4 of the 1999 World

Series was not the time to play the baseball equivalent of "whose is longer."

"He was a completely different pitcher," Jones said. "That's a testament to his ability to learn from prior at bats. He knows I'm a good fastball hitter. He knows that most times I'm sitting dead red and he fed me a steady diet of off-speed stuff in the World Series. He wasn't going to let me hurt him and I didn't. He kept throwing me the split, but he kept throwing me the split for a strike. You have to respect the 94–95 miles per hour fastball because guys like me don't want to get beat with the fastball. He kept throwing me splits down in the zone and I kept beating them into the ground."

If you didn't know anything about Clemens's past and were seeing him in Game 4 for the first time, you'd think you were seeing a groundball artist at work, like a Tommy John or, to be more contemporary, a Derek Lowe type. Clemens recorded 16 ground ball outs in his 7⅔ innings of work in that game. Jones didn't have a particularly good postseason overall, hitting .244 across the three series, with just a home run against El Duque in Game 1 and 4 RBIs. He killed many a worm against Clemens, grounding to shortstop, back to Clemens, and to third in his three at bats against the starter. Then, for good measure, he grounded out to second against closer Mariano Rivera with runners on the corners with two outs and down 3–1 to end the eighth inning.

"Especially as you get older, you want to become more efficient," Jones said about Clemens's evolution as a pitcher. "You want to pitch more to contact as opposed to striking ten–twelve people out. The thing about it is you can save a little in the tank, pitch to contact if you have a good defense behind you, which they did. If you do get in a jam, you still have that extra gear to get the big strikeout when you need to."

Clemens needed just four strikeouts before giving way to Rivera, who retired all four batters he faced to be on the mound for the final out of a title-clinching game. He was the Series MVP after winning 1 game and saving 2 others, but he wasn't alone. Rivera didn't give up a single run in the 1999 postseason, but neither did Jeff Nelson, nor, in a lesser role, Mike Stanton.

Just looking at the career ERAs for Yankee relievers in the postseason provides another reason why the starters, Clemens included, had the confidence to just go out and pitch and not worry about much more than that. If they kept the Yankees in the game and handed a lead, however small, over to the pen, it pretty much was over during the string of championships. Nelson had 16 wins and a 2.65 ERA in the postseason, with all but eleven of his fifty-five appearances coming with the Yankees. He had a 1.69 ERA in five World Series. Stanton began showing his postseason acumen with the Braves early on and has 10 wins and a 2.10 career ERA in the playoffs. He, too, was stingier in the World Series, lowering that ERA to 1.54 in twenty games. Then there's Rivera, perhaps the best postseason reliever of all time. In seventy games, Rivera has 8 wins, 34 saves, and a ridiculous 0.77 ERA. Think it was demoralizing for the Braves to have to claw back into the '99 Series against Clemens? With each passing inning, it got more and more dire, because they knew once the relief corps took over, they were in trouble.

"During the whole Yankee run, they had the innate ability to shorten the game," Jones said. "You knew if you were losing after the sixth or seventh inning, you weren't going to put too much together against their bullpen. They had righties, lefties, power arms, guys who got you out. That was a big reason for their success."

Jones and the Braves did get an opportunity to exact at least a little revenge the following season in interleague play. Clemens was a bit more like himself in 2000, and while his numbers on the surface don't look extraordinary, he did finish sixth in the Cy Young Award voting. His 3.70 ERA was second best in the American League that year, way behind the 1.74 mark of Cy Young Award winner Pedro Martinez. Hitters managed just a .236 average and he was back over the 200-inning mark after a one-year hiatus. He may have been becoming a more efficient pitcher, but he still finished fifth in the league in strikeouts with 188.

Jones was having another All-Star season, perhaps not as breathtaking as his 1999 campaign, but it was good enough for another Sliver Slugger Award. He'd finish the year hitting .311 with 36 homers and 111 RBIs. Much as he had been before their meeting back in 1997, Jones was just truly heating up when they met in 2000 for the first time since the World Series. Jones would hit .385 in June that year with 8 homers and 24 RBIs.

The two teams met in Atlanta right at the beginning of the month. Even though Jones homered in the eighth inning off Jeff Nelson in the opener, it was the Yankees who ended any hopes of payback with a 5–2 victory behind El Duque. Then it was Clemens's turn on a Saturday afternoon. It was one of those marquee matchups again, Clemens versus Maddux, that always creates a ton of hype. (A few years later, the duo would pair up twice in a rare battle between 300-game winners.) Even though they hadn't reached that magic number yet, there was still quite a bit of anticipation for the game.

Ever go to see a summer blockbuster movie, one you've been dying to see for months? Everyone's been talking about it, the buzz is palpable, you wait in line for hours to see it, and then the movie is a clunker? That's pretty much what happened on June 3, 2000. "There was a bunch of hype, Maddux and Clemens," Jones recalled. "Everyone's expecting it to be a 2–1 or 3–2 game. It turned out to be a slugfest coming down to the ninth inning. Make no mistake, I don't think there's a guy across baseball who won't tell you he [Clemens] and Maddux, during our era, are the best pitchers bar none. All I can say is we caught him on a bad day."

Indeed. Clemens gave up 6 runs, 4 earned, on 6 hits and 4 walks over five innings of work. Maddux wasn't any better, allowing 13 hits and 7 runs over 5⅔ innings pitched. Neither figured into the decision and the Braves went on to win, 11–7. Jones went 1 for 2 with an RBI and a run scored, though he did pick up his first strikeout against Clemens in regular-season play.

And that was it for another four years. Even though the Braves and Yankees were perennial play-off teams from 2000 to 2003, the Braves couldn't get past the NLCS in any of those seasons. The Yankees won it all again in 2000, but that was the last time they did so. They lost in the Fall Classic to the Diamondbacks and Marlins, and never got another crack at the Braves. It wasn't until Clemens decided to "unretire" for the first time and join the Astros in 2004 that the two met on the field again.

It was far from an inconsequential meeting. Heading into the game on August 3, 2004, Clemens and the Astros were just one game over .500, but they were also only five games out of the wild card lead. Jones and the Braves had a 5½-game lead over the Phillies atop the NL East and were headed to their thirteenth straight division title. Clemens didn't figure into the decision, though he certainly did his part. The Rocket went seven-plus innings, allowing just 2 runs, 1 of which was earned. He also held Jones in check. The third baseman had a down year in 2004, hitting a career-low .248 and falling short of 100 RBIs for the first time since 1995, as he missed twenty-five games due to injury. He was much more productive in the second half of the season, but Clemens stopped him for at least one game, striking out Jones twice, but not with the hard stuff.

"There was a lot more finesse," said Jones, who did walk and score in his first plate appearance. "He was less willing to challenge hitters, but he was still effective. There was the split and the development of the cutter. The last couple of years, he's been a completely different pitcher. Obviously, he can still paint the 93, 94 on the outside corner, but he's developing a backdoor cutter, where if he falls behind in the count, he can paint that on the outside corner, which locks up a lot of hitters. Always in the back of your mind now, you better have that split. You have to make him throw it up in the zone. If it starts just above the knees, you're out."

Clemens recorded quite a few outs when the two teams met in the National League Division Series that year. While the Braves were the favorites after a ninety-six-win season and a division title, the Astros weren't a weak wild card team by any definition. Houston won ninety-two games during the regular season, meaning the club went 38–18 following that early August game that Clemens started against the Braves, including its last seven games to pass the Cubs and the Giants and take the wild card lead. Clemens had anchored the staff, and would go on to win his unprecedented seventh Cy Young Award. Still, with the first two games, and Game 5 if necessary, at Turner Field in Atlanta, most predicted the Braves would advance to the NLCS.

The Astros had different ideas and Clemens helped them get off on the right foot. While his typically outstanding command went AWOL—he walked 6 and threw 2 wild pitches—he went seven strong innings, allowing 3 runs (2 earned) while striking out 7. The Houston offense jumped all over Jaret Wright and the Astros put an end to any Atlanta home-field advantage with a 9–3 victory. Jones, who followed up a torrid August, during which he hit .337 with 11 homers and 29 RBIs, with an awful September/October

(.227, 5, 23), went 0 for 3 with a walk and a couple of strikeouts against Clemens.

The Braves bounced back with a thrilling 4–2, eleven-inning victory in Game 2 to salvage a split as the series headed to Houston. The Astros grabbed the series edge with an 8–5 victory, needing just one win in two games to advance. The Braves, playoff-tested as they were, weren't quite ready to capitulate. They jumped all over Clemens in Game 4, scoring five times in the second inning. Atlanta's pitching couldn't hold the lead and it wasn't until the ninth that the Braves eked out a 6–5 victory to send everyone back to Atlanta for a winner-takes-all contest.

Houston jumped out to an early 3–0 lead in that Game 5 behind ace Roy Oswalt. The Braves managed to score twice in the fifth, but when the Astros added a five-spot in the seventh, that was all she wrote. It was Atlanta's third consecutive five-game NLDS loss.

Jones went 1 for 2 against Clemens in Game 4, but his series performance matched his overall season: disappointing. He went just 4 for 20 with nary an extra-base hit to be shown for the effort.

The 2004 meetings between Jones and Clemens may have been interesting, but they were merely an opening act for what was to come in 2005. Anyone in Houston on April 18 should have gotten an inkling that it was going to be a very interesting year. It was another campaign cut short by injuries for Jones, who suffered a foot injury that allowed him to play in just 109 games. The injury hadn't yet occurred in mid-April, and Jones went 3 for 4 in the game, including a couple of hits against Clemens.

It was about all the offense in the game. Clemens went seven scoreless innings and struck out 8. In his first four starts of 2005—this one being the second—the Rocket gave up just a single earned run over twenty-eight innings while striking out 32. Amazingly, he only got one win to show for it. Part of it was lack of offensive support and some of it was terrific pitching by the opponent. On April 18, that was Tim Hudson, who went nine scoreless innings, yet also walked away from the game empty-handed. The outcome wasn't decided until Ryan Langerhans homered in the top of the twelfth inning to give the Braves a 1–0 win in the frenzied atmosphere at Houston's Minute Maid Park. Going back to that 1993 rehab start, Jones had seen Clemens in various stages of his career over the previous thirteen years and he couldn't come up with an outing that bested this one.

"In that ballpark, when the roof is closed, it's awfully loud," Jones said. "Clemens being a Texas boy, they got geeked up and filled that place every time he was on the mound. He was about as good as I've seen him that night. Luckily, our pitcher was equal to the task.

"While you always look forward to facing a first-ballot Hall of Famer, you know you have your hands full. I've never had somebody like Clemens—I made this statement to [Astros first baseman] Jeff Bagwell before when I got on first base—he makes you work so hard during an at bat just to make contact, to put the ball in fair territory. If you get on base or get a base hit, you feel like you just hit a home run. At the end of the game, you're so mentally drained because you're trying to think along with him, trying to work so hard to play a chess match with him. More times than not, he wins."

He won a huge one, and not when most would expect it, in another wild National League Division Series between the two clubs. The Braves, of course, won the NL East, though their ninety wins represented their second-lowest win total in their fourteen-year run that would finally end in 2006. The Astros were only one game worse, with eighty-nine victories, enough to get them another wild card appearance, barely edging out the Phillies. Clemens won only thirteen games during the regular season, a big reason he finished third in Cy Young voting despite the fact that in many ways he was better than he was in 2004 and statistically trumped the pitchers who finished ahead of him, Chris Carpenter and Dontrelle Willis.

Jones looked like he was destined to have a terrific postseason in Game 1, when he doubled and homered, driving in a pair of runs. It was his thirteenth postseason home run and ninth in NLDS play. The latter is an all-time record in the relatively brief history of that extra round of playoffs. Unfortunately for the Braves, it wasn't nearly enough offense to offset the Astros' banging out 10 runs on 11 hits against Tim Hudson and relievers. Jones didn't do much for the rest of the series, finishing with a .176 average in seventeen at bats.

Once again, home-field advantage was thrown out the window and once again, the Braves managed to salvage a split by winning Game 2. John Smoltz went seven outstanding innings, allowing just an earned run while the Braves were able to figure out Clemens this time around. They scored 3 runs in the second and a couple of more in the third, the big blow a three-run homer from catcher Brian McCann. Clemens went just five innings total, allowing the 5 runs on 6 hits and getting collared with the loss.

Getting Clemens out of the game early at the time certainly seemed like a good thing to the Braves. It would turn out, though, that the Astros would find the silver lining in that cloud late in Game 4. Back in Houston, the Astros took Game 3 behind Roy Oswalt and were facing an eerily similar situation to the previous year. They were determined not to have to go back to Atlanta for a Game 5. It just took them eighteen innings to get it done.

The Braves jumped out to an early 4–0 lead and had a 6–1 advantage in the eighth. But the Astros scored four times in the bottom of that frame on a Lance Berkman grand slam, then sent the game into extra innings on Brad Ausmus's solo shot in the ninth. Then what ostensibly was the nightcap of a doubleheader ensued, and it was a pitcher's battle. Both teams had some opportunities with runners in scoring position, but a host of relievers kept the offenses from pushing a run across.

A buzz filled Minute Maid Park when there was action in the Astros bullpen as the game approached the fifteenth inning. Roger Clemens was getting loose. He'd be coming in on just two days rest—almost three because of the length of this game. But because he'd been chased early, he'd thrown only ninety-two pitches in that loss. "You don't know how things are going to work out," Jones said. "We felt good about how we approached him and swung the bats the first time around. Unfortunately, he came back to haunt us later on."

Because of a lack of position players, Clemens actually pinch-hit for reliever Dan Wheeler in the bottom of the fifteenth and struck out. Then he came into the game in the top of the sixteenth. He certainly didn't look worn out, striking out two of the first three batters he faced. "It doesn't matter with him," said Jones, thinking back with respect. "Even if he doesn't have the rest he needs, he can still fall back on the finesse part of the game to get you out. He doesn't have to throw you 95-mile-per-hour, four-seam heaters. He can sink it. He can cut it. I can't emphasize enough how much the splitter has done for his career."

Despite knowing that, Jones admits he wasn't exactly prepared to see Clemens up and throwing in the bullpen in that game. Once he did, he knew the Braves had their work cut out for them. "I was a little surprised," Jones admitted. "I knew they really didn't want to go back to Atlanta, so they were pulling out all the stops. You're already pretty tired; it's been a long game. To have him coming out of the bullpen, you know it's not going to get any easier. It's a little demoralizing at that point because you know you might get one chance at him. If you don't make the most of it, chances are he's going to shut the rest of your lineup down. That's what he did. He did what an unbelievable pitcher does. He shut us down and gave his offense the opportunity to win it late."

Jones got one chance at Clemens in the top of the eighteenth inning. He grounded out to second as Clemens pitched around an error to send the game to the bottom of the inning still tied, 6–6. He likely would have kept going, at least for a little while, after leading off the Astros turn at bat by striking out. But Chris Burke made sure that wouldn't be necessary, ending the longest game in postseason history with a home run off of Joey Devine to send the Astros to the NLCS. Amazingly after that marathon, Houston had enough left in the tank to beat the Cardinals and make it to their first World Series, where they were promptly swept by the White Sox.

Had the Astros won the World Series that year, perhaps Clemens would have officially called it quits. It turned out the tank was empty by Fall Classic time and the White Sox swept the Astros to win their first title since 1917. Clemens started Game 1 of that series but was forced to depart after two innings with a sore hamstring. So instead of hanging them up, he came back in June of 2006 to try to get Houston back into the postseason. While that effort would fall just short, it did allow Jones to try one last time to master the master. It came near the end of the season, a lost one for the Atlanta Braves. They would not be headed to the postseason for the first time in a decade and a half. Jones once again had some injury problems and played in only 110 games. He was extremely productive when he was on the field, hitting .324 and slugging .596.

Jones had missed two weeks in the beginning of September, but came back to try to salvage the season.

He did finish with a bit of a flourish, going 10 for 24 with 3 homers over his final nine games. The final series of the year was against the Astros, and it was surprisingly crucial for Houston. Left for dead earlier in the month—they were 8½ games behind the Cardinals, with the Reds in front of them in second—and six games under .500 through September 19. The Astros then proceeded to win nine straight heading into the series against Atlanta. At the same time the Cardinals had collapsed and the Astros were just a half-game out.

Things seemed to be set up perfectly for Houston. Clemens was pitching the opener against a Braves team that surely had pride, but also likely had one foot out the door at that point. The forty-four-year-old Rocket had won two games in that winning streak, giving up just a run in eleven innings. He certainly wasn't bad on September 29 in Atlanta. He went six innings, allowing 6 hits and 2 runs (only 1 of which was earned), while striking out 7. It's just that young lefty Chuck James was a tiny bit better. The twenty-four-year-old southpaw yielded just a run over seven innings as the Braves went on to win, 4–1. The loss, coupled with the Cardinals win that night, put the Astros 1½ games behind. The Cardinals won the following afternoon, ending Houston's improbable dream.

It seemed like it could be the end of Clemens's twenty-three-year dream as well. At least the folks on hand at Turner Field thought so. So did the Braves third baseman, who went 1 for 4 in the game, though the hit—a home run—came off of reliever Fernando

Nieve in the eighth. When Chris Burke came up to pinch hit for Clemens in the seventh inning, the Braves faithful got on their feet until the Rocket came out for what many thought would be the final curtain call of his career.

"I really did. I thought that was going to be his last one," Jones said. "When he came out of the game, the fans in Atlanta stood up and gave him a standing ovation. I was standing on third base, clapping, trying to get everyone going to get him to come out and give a curtain call. I thought that was it. Fortunately, it wasn't."

It might be, however, the last time Jones will ever get to face Clemens. The Braves didn't play the Yankees in interleague play in 2007 and Clemens made another late return to the big leagues. If this is indeed the end—and one should never say never when Roger Clemens is involved—Jones can look back with a certain amount of pride. He went a respectable 5 for 16 against Clemens in regular-season matchups for a .313 average to go along with that lone home run in Toronto back in 1997. The postseason was a little tougher, but there's certainly no shame in being retired by Roger Clemens and Jones knows that one dinger will go a long way when he's done playing the game and has time to reflect.

"I've gotten my hits, but it takes [a toll]," Jones said. "You can't just take your hacks against Roger Clemens. You have to be a pretty cerebral hitter. Cerebral hitters will get their hits off of him. Guys who go up there without a game plan against him [and aren't] willing to change that game plan from pitch to pitch, or at bat to at bat, he's going to dominate. Those are the guys he dominates. Fortunately, for me, I've tried to vary my approach against him and it's worked out somewhat.

"Twenty, thirty years down the road, when they say who were the toughest pitchers you ever faced, Roger Clemens is going to be right at the top. I know they're going to ask me, 'Did you ever hit a home run off of him?' And I'm going to be able to say, 'Yes.' Make no mistake about it, in the fight between the two of us, he's had the upper hand."

In the end, though, it wasn't any of the on-field confrontations Jones will cherish when he thinks about Roger Clemens. Instead, he'll look back at the one time he was Clemens's teammate. The United States may not have come away with the World Baseball Classic title, but that did nothing to take away from the experience Jones had as the third baseman with Clemens on the mound.

"I got to play behind him at the Classic, twice. I loved every minute of it," Jones said. "It was awesome to be the guy standing behind him instead of the guy at the plate. I got to see how his teammates have felt playing behind him for so long. It was a big thrill of mine."

Not as big a thrill, it turns out, as the aftermath. For all of the thrills Jones has shared with Clemens, both as an opponent and then briefly as a teammate, the one thing that might stand out the most was the few hours he got to spend with Clemens and another future Hall of Famer after the WBC was over.

"After we lost in the World Baseball Classic, he and Derek Jeter came up to me and asked if I wanted to fly home with them, to Tampa, because our Spring Training sites were so close," Jones recounted. "That flight from California to Tampa was awesome. It was a career highlight in and of itself and it wasn't even on a baseball field. Just getting to sit there and talk— we share a lot of the same interests off the field—I'll remember that plane flight as much as some of the head-to-head battles we've had over the years."

Thinking back on that conversation, very little of which was about baseball, Jones realizes there were definite clues about Clemens's future. They talked about family and hunting, things off the field, for a reason. Ever the competitor, Clemens wasn't ready to let his guard down just yet. Jones should have realized that was a sign the Rocket was preparing for at least one more go-round.

"I think he always knew in the back of his mind, he wasn't quite done yet," Jones said with a smile. "He wasn't going to divulge anything I might be able to use against him later."

DARRYL **HAMILTON** (2000)

"THERE WAS NO INTENT."

That phrase was uttered endlessly by Roger Clemens following Game 2 of the 2000 World Series in response to one of the most surreal events in Fall Classic history. Whether you believe it speaks to the very essence of baseball allegiances in New York. Yankee fans will likely say to their graves that there's no way their pitcher meant any harm. Those who call the Mets their team, however, probably will never buy that explanation.

The incident, which most agreed immediately after the fact would likely overshadow the entire Series (that has proven to be correct) involved Clemens, Mets catcher Mike Piazza, and a sawed-off bat in the first inning of Game 2. The CliffsNotes version goes something like this: Facing Clemens in the first inning of the second game of the World Series, Piazza broke his bat in half fouling off a Clemens fastball. The jagged edge of the bat flew out at the pitcher, who promptly picked it up and threw it at Piazza. A stare down occurred, peace was restored, and no one was thrown out of the game. Clemens went on to throw

eight shutout innings, the Yankees won their four-
teenth straight World Series game and went on to win
the Subway Series, ultimately, in five games.

To this day even witnesses in the dugout can't be
sure what took place that night at Yankee Stadium.
Darryl Hamilton was a reserve outfielder for the
Mets and had the perfect vantage point from the
Mets bench. He had twelve years of big-league experience to draw from, thirty at bats over a decade
against the Rocket, and a developing friendship with
his fellow Houston resident from which to gain some
perspective. But like just about anyone else who was
at the game or watched it on TV, his explanation can
truly only be guesswork.

"I couldn't understand what had happened,"
Hamilton admitted. "It was surreal in the fact that not
only did he break Piazza's bat, but the bat came flying
right back at him. He catches it on one hop and fires it
right back. To me that is something that will happen
again sometime in the Year 3040. It just doesn't happen like that. The only thing I could think of was that
maybe he thought the bat was being thrown at him.
I've never asked him what he was thinking about. I'm
just assuming with all the hype, with all the talk about
what was going to happen in the game, for him to be
so locked and throw a pitch and all of a sudden see a
bat coming at him, maybe he assumed Piazza threw
the bat at him, trying to get him back for before.
That's the only thing I can think of. It was crazy, it
was off the charts, to say the least."

To truly understand why this was such a big deal,
other than that it took place on the game's biggest

stage in the largest media market in the country, it's important to have some of the background for context. Mike Piazza, who declined to be interviewed for this book, hit Roger Clemens very well. Of course, the future Hall of Fame backstop hit many pitchers well, the reason he'll have a plaque in Cooperstown one day, some would say ironically near Clemens assuming they retire at around the same time. But his success against Clemens was striking, compared with how the right-hander dominated most other hitters. In a total of 19 at bats in his career, Piazza had 8 hits off of the Rocket, for a .421 average. Half of those hits were home runs. At the time of the World Series matchup, Piazza was 7 for 12 against the right-hander, with 3 homers.

"One thing about Piazza, when he's in a good groove, there's nobody better," said Hamilton, who played with Piazza in New York from 1999 to 2001. "He obviously felt comfortable against Clemens. He was seeing the ball really well against him and anything he threw up there, he was all over. We were all waiting for Clemens to do something to get him off the plate."

Evidently, July 8, 2000, was the time to do it. It was an interleague game, the nightcap in an odd day-night doubleheader. The first game, which was played at Shea Stadium, was won by the Yankees. The teams then moved to Yankee Stadium for the second game, with Clemens on the hill. Piazza, who was DHing in the American League ballpark, led off the second inning of a scoreless game. Clemens hit Piazza in the head with a fastball, knocking him down and out of the game. It forced him to miss his eighth consecutive All-Star Game. Not that the Yankees-Mets rivalry needed any more stoking, but the beaning would turn the simmer up to a high flame; the rivalry would boil over in October.

Hamilton, who would play just one more season in 2001 before calling it a career, spent most of the 2000 season on the disabled list. But he was with the team on that summer day, and while he's absolutely sure Clemens wanted to brush Piazza back, maybe even knock him down, he doesn't think he was looking to plunk him and knock him into next week. That doesn't mean, of course, that everyone in the Mets dugout wasn't ready to storm the field to back up their star player.

"I don't know any major-league pitcher out there who looks at a player who's hit him well and says to himself, 'You know what, I'm going to hit him in the head. I'm going to hit him in the head so he doesn't do it again,'" Hamilton said. "I found it hard to believe that he was trying to hurt Piazza. What he was trying to do, which I figured he would do sooner or later, was get him off of the plate.

"It was crazy for a good ten seconds. You had twenty guys in the dugout who were ready to go on the field and go after Clemens. It was weird, we were in Yankee Stadium, and everybody in the dugout was very upset that our best player had been knocked down, hit in the head, and basically was laying there. Once things settled down and Mike got up and they brought him into the clubhouse, then cooler heads prevailed."

Interestingly enough, while the Mets were incensed that Clemens had beaned Piazza, some were hoping there would have been more of a response from their All-Star catcher, even though due to the severity of the blow, there wasn't much Piazza could have done in this instance. That being said, it may have been something the Mets stored in the back of their minds and it resurfaced big time when the teams met again in the World Series.

"There were a lot of guys who were upset about how things went down," Hamilton said. "For the most part a lot of guys were a little upset at Piazza, believe it or not. A lot of guys felt he should've known something was coming and the fact he didn't do anything about it was a little upsetting. To defend Piazza, he had just been hit in the head with a 95-mile-per-hour fastball, so there wasn't a lot he could've done. But it got really magnified in the World Series."

The magnifying glass was out long before Piazza's bat sailed out to the Yankee Stadium pitching mound. Before the Series even started, the impending Clemens-Piazza showdown was all anyone wanted to talk about. A Subway Series, the first time two New York teams met in the Fall Classic since the Yankees and Dodgers battled in 1956, evidently wasn't enough to stir the pot for the city's media. The rest of the country may have been ho-humming the all-New York matchup, but it should have provided plenty of drama for anyone who was interested. Instead, the specter of a rematch between pitcher and hitter took center stage.

At the start of the Series, Clemens apologized for having plunked Piazza, claiming that he never intended to actually hit the catcher. Piazza told reporters he had put it behind him and that it wasn't relevant to the Series, which was supposed to be all about who was going to win. Mets manager Bobby Valentine said, "If anybody thinks it's the most important thing going on, they're incorrect. If they think it is forgotten about, they're also incorrect." Yankee manager Joe Torre also tried to shift focus away from Clemens versus Piazza II when he said, "I think it's a disservice to people what's going on. Whenever you pick up a newspaper, whatever network you watch, that's all you see is Mike getting hit in the head. I would like to believe this World Series is more about competition and fun than about getting even and inciting riots."

Sure, everyone would like to believe that. But especially in the cauldron that is New York, Clemens-Piazza was too juicy a storyline to pass up. Of course the teams actually had to play Game 1 before the script could be played out in the second game. If it weren't for the "bat incident," the Series may have been remembered for its opening stanza more than anything else.

Clocking in at four hours and fifty-one minutes, it turned out to be the longest World Series game, in terms of time, in history. At twelve innings there was only one game longer by that measure and it had taken place back in 1916. A pitcher's duel featuring a pair of lefties, Al Leiter and Andy Pettitte, it remained scoreless into the sixth inning when the Yankees took a 2–0 lead as they attempted to win their third consecutive title. The Mets fought back and actually took the lead with a three-run seventh only to see the lead disappear in the bottom of the ninth on a Chuck Knoblauch sacrifice fly off closer Armando Benitez. It was unlikely hero Jose Vizcaino who singled in the winning run in the bottom of the twelfth to give the Yankees a 1–0 lead. Hamilton recalled an odd vibe in the Mets clubhouse heading into the Series, one that certainly didn't change with the disheartening loss.

"We went into the World Series thinking we had a better team the year before, but we didn't get there," Hamilton said. "I think we were happy, obviously, to be in the World Series, but we weren't so locked that we were saying we could win it. I know that's weird to hear, but I think that's just the way a lot of guys were thinking. Especially after losing the first game the way we did, it really kind of brought a downer to the way we were going. If we win Game 1, obviously, the intensity turns around."

Don't misunderstand Hamilton. It's not that the Mets weren't giving maximum effort in trying to win the Series. Oddly, in a hyped series like this one against the Yankees, they actually felt kind of loose. The Mets were the underdogs, if there could be one in a matchup of two powerhouses like this. The Yankees had everything on the line; the Mets had virtually nothing.

"We felt we were good enough to play with the Yankees," Hamilton explained. "We understood the Yankees couldn't lose to us. That was one thing to our advantage. We knew they had to win. We could go out, we could play well, and if we lost, people would say, 'Well, they gave it a good try.' But the

Yankees couldn't lose to us. [Yankee owner George] Steinbrenner would go nuts. It's a Yankees town right now. The pressure was squarely on them. That goes back to Game 1. If we put more pressure on them, then things change."

What that would have done to the Game 2 craziness is almost unimaginable. How differently would the incident have been viewed if the Yankees were in a 1–0 deficit at home instead of up a game? It's a question, obviously, that never can be answered. Neither can the one about what precisely happened on the field that night. Clemens, after the fact, stated he was very emotional, picked up the bat and fired it toward the batboy, not seeing Piazza there down the first baseline. Whatever the reasoning, Hamilton had a pretty good idea of what Clemens meant by saying, "There was no intent," even if he'll never truly understand what he witnessed.

"I don't know if he went out there and said to himself, 'What if something happens? I'm going to take on Piazza.' I don't think he did that," Hamilton said. "But if you have a bat coming right at you and your mind-set is maybe he threw this bat at me, first thing you're going to do is throw it back. That's the only logic I can put on the situation to try to explain it.

"It was the craziest thing I've ever seen. Very rarely, in a situation like that with all the hype, in New York, with the Subway Series, the fact that the interleague series was so nuts with Piazza getting hit in the head, there was so much talk about how something was going to go down, for something like that to happen, to me it was off the charts, I couldn't believe it."

Like with the beaning back in July, many of the Mets couldn't believe Piazza's reaction, or lack thereof, as much as they couldn't fathom what Clemens had done. This time, though, Piazza didn't have being knocked out as a defense for not retaliating in some fashion, leading some teammates to be more angry about the fact that he didn't charge the mound. Instead, Piazza motioned to Clemens and yelled, "What's your problem?" Later, he would state that he didn't want to get thrown out of the World Series. As the team's best hitter, there was definite validity to that attitude, but most of the Mets would have preferred a different response.

"A lot of guys on the team were highly upset and not necessarily at Clemens, but at Piazza for not doing anything," Hamilton said. "Lenny Harris was the worst, he was just wearing him out over that. A lot of guys were thinking, 'We understand it's the World Series, but you know what? Sometimes you have to do what you have to do.' The fact that he's already been hit by a fastball in the head, knocked unconscious, then the first time facing him in the World Series, he's got a bat coming right back at him. Sometimes, you have to look at the situation and say, 'Guys, I'm sorry, but I had to take care of business.' And that's what a lot of guys in the clubhouse were saying. And looking back at it, if Piazza takes him out, maybe we have a chance to win. But it didn't happen."

The Mets did mount a furious comeback, scoring five times in the ninth inning only to fall short by a run. It should be noted that Piazza homered in that inning to put the Mets on the scoreboard, something that wouldn't have happened had he ventured out to the mound to confront Clemens back in the first. Hamilton's point, of course, is that Clemens would have been out of the game and not twirling perhaps his best World Series gem, allowing just 2 hits and no walks while striking out 9 over eight innings.

Hamilton had the misfortune of being asked to pinch-hit later in the game. He had picked up just 105 at bats over forty-three games during the regular season. He got just six more in the first two rounds of the postseason, and when he was called upon to hit with one out in the eighth inning, that was his first plate appearance of the Series. At the very least he did have several years of back records to draw from for the at bat against Clemens.

The first time Hamilton stepped into the box against Roger Clemens was in July 1991. Then, Hamilton was a twenty-six-year-old outfielder establishing himself in the Milwaukee Brewers lineup. The 1991 season was the first in which he was an everyday player and he hit .311 with 16 stolen bases. He was a confident young hitter, but it was something different completely to try and hit Clemens, who went on to win his third Cy Young Award that season. Hamilton is the first to admit that like so many young hitters have, he got caught up in the Rocket aura early on.

"The times I faced him early in my career, I think they were more in situations where I was in awe of him," said Hamilton, who added that this was before the two had struck up their friendship. "All the things he had done, winning a national championship at the

University of Texas, doing all those great things with Boston, striking out 20. I was in awe. It was one of those deals where you get to the plate, you try to get your emotions together and not get caught up in the moment and focus on getting a pitch to hit. But it's almost like facing Nolan Ryan. You see him and you can't believe you're facing him."

It was even worse in Boston. The buzz at Fenway Park when Clemens was doing his thing there was much different than on other days. Those too young to understand may recall what Fenway was like when Pedro Martinez took the mound. Clemens was the precursor of that, and for young players coming into that den, it wasn't always so easy to deal with, even if they had the presence of mind to appreciate how special it was. "You try to settle your emotions, but it's hard to do," Hamilton said. "It was a different environment in Fenway Park when he pitched. It was very easy for the visiting team to get caught up in those emotions.

"It was pretty cool. I remember one time, when I was in the on-deck circle and I was leading off that game, I can definitely remember them playing Elton John's 'Rocket Man' as he warmed up. I'm looking around the ballpark and it's a packed house and I'm sitting there thinking, 'This is pretty cool. It doesn't get any better than this.'"

Hamilton had thirty at bats between 1991 and 1996 to try and get the better of Clemens, but found only limited success. His career line shows a .200 average (6 for 20) against the Rocket with a pair of doubles and four strikeouts. There were some in

Boston who thought Clemens was nearing the end by that 1996 season, but Hamilton knew otherwise. Perhaps he lost a tick or two on the fastball, but a drop in velocity does not necessarily mean a pitcher is heading toward the washed-up pile.

"When you face a legend and they are so dominant for so many years and they maybe lose a couple of miles per hour on their fastball, that's a break for a hitter," Hamilton explained. "They're used to a guy just blowing them away. If they have a small chance now to go up there and hit, a lot of people think that means they're losing their stuff and that's not necessarily true.

"Sometimes you have to reinvent yourself. What Clemens has done well is he hasn't relied on his fastball that much in the so-called twilight of his career. He's focused on being a more complete pitcher. A lot of the great pitchers do that. When you come in the league, a lot of these guys are coming in throwing 95–96 miles per hour, blowing away guys, and it's not really that difficult for them. As they get older, that stuff starts to tone down a little bit, that fastball slows down a little bit, but the mind is still there. A lot of the great pitchers will make adjustments. You have to do that and Clemens has done that better than anyone else out there."

Hamilton moved to the National League for the 1997 season and didn't have to dig in against Clemens again until the 2000 World Series. Still, he saw enough in how Clemens was approaching his craft to know he would figure out a way to continue dominating hitters even if he couldn't do so as frequently with the high heater. As much as coming up with new pitches, as Clemens did with the split-fingered fastball when he was in Toronto, Hamilton thinks the key to the Rocket's success has been his ability to continuously use his mound presence to his advantage.

"He had everything working for him in that sense. He knew how to pitch and he was so intimidating," Hamilton said. "I point at Clemens and I point at Nolan Ryan as two guys who, from day one, hadn't lost anything as far as intimidation factor. If you can have that when you don't have your great stuff, that sometimes gets you over the top. That gets you through those games when you don't have that great command."

To that end Clemens has never been afraid to move a hitter off the plate when he deemed it necessary. Perhaps the definition of necessity can be debated, but one of the things that has made Clemens so consistently dominant has been his ability to dictate terms from the mound. If he felt a hitter was getting too comfortable in the box, it was his job to reclaim the plate. If the way to beat a young hitter was to introduce him to a fastball up in the zone to rattle him, then that's what had to be done.

Hamilton is not a guy to take things personally on the field. Even before he got to know Clemens off the field, he understood what the right-hander was trying to accomplish. It came into sharper focus as their friendship evolved. Hamilton saw his share of chin music courtesy of Clemens, but never thought much of it. "You can't take anything personally with him when you're playing against him on the field," Hamilton said. "What I mean by that, if he knocks you down, gets you off the plate, or whatever, you can't take it personally. You can't take it as if he's trying to hurt you. What he's trying to do is beat you. I can respect any pitcher who I'm friends with; I understand they have a job to do. I don't look at it as if they're out to get me. I look at it as if they're trying to be better than me that time at the plate. My goal is to try to be better than him.

"He's knocked me down a few times and I've gotten up and laughed about it. It's ticked me off, but I'm focused on trying to get him. Any pitcher knocks me down, I'm trying to get him after that, but the fact we see each other in the off-season, we work out every once in a while together, I'm really trying to get him just like he's trying to get me. There's a little bit of bragging rights involved with that."

It turns out it's not just baseball where that kind of trash talking could go on. Hamilton and Clemens have become closer friends particularly over the past several years since Hamilton and his family moved into the same Houston neighborhood as the Clemenses. The initial bond was formed around two players understanding what it takes to play the game of baseball at the highest level and it's grown from there.

"Everyone who's played Major League Baseball understands, for the most part, how difficult it is to get to that level, so I think there's a little bit of respect for all of the guys who have made it and a little bit of a friendship as well," Hamilton said. "Playing against him and knowing that we both live in Houston and

we're both not too far from each other, we both became a little bit closer as the years went by."

A good part of the relationship has been developed on the golf course. Hamilton admits Clemens is
the better of the two on the links, but that he's not
that far behind. That has led to some spirited competition. Anyone who thinks Clemens is laid-back when
he's not between the white lines hasn't seen him on
the course. "He's intense off the field in the same
way," Hamilton said. "Obviously, off the field he's
not as locked on what he's trying to do. But, whatever he does out there, he's still very intense and he
wants to be the best. It doesn't change, as far as I'm
concerned. Facing him and playing with him on the
golf course are all the same to me."

Four years passed between opportunities for
Hamilton to face him on the baseball field and the
pinch-hitting appearance in Game 2 of the 2000 World
Series would be the last time the two would meet in
such a manner. Clemens had a 5–0 lead and was in
his last inning of masterful work. Hamilton knew
he'd have his work cut out for him, coming cold off
the bench against a guy who was clearly on a roll.

With the lead he had and the ease with which
he was dominating the Mets lineup, it would be
easy to assume that Clemens wouldn't even pause
upon seeing Hamilton stride to the plate. Hamilton
had had a strong 1999 season between the Rockies
and Mets but had barely played in 2000. Not that
Clemens would take any big-league hitter lightly,
particularly in the World Series, but most would
think he'd be toeing the rubber ready to continue

dealing the second Hamilton was announced as the pinch hitter for shortstop Mike Bordick.

That wasn't what happened. Clemens stepped off and summoned catcher Jorge Posada to the mound. There wasn't anyone on base, so this wasn't a case of them needing to change up signs. With all due respect to Hamilton, they didn't need to carefully discuss the game plan against such a dangerous hitter or even a guy who'd had a lot of success against Clemens over the years. So just what did Clemens so urgently need to tell his catcher at that instant?

"He told me what happened in the off-season. That's how I know the story," Hamilton said. "He basically told Posada, 'I can't let him get a hit off of me. If he gets a hit off of me, he's going to be wearing me out the whole off-season. We have to get him.' I thought that was hilarious. It was funny he was thinking about that."

Hamilton, for his part, was thinking about a fastball. He figured his only shot was to take a hack at a fastball early and hope he got it, knowing that he wasn't going to get many hittable pitches and that if he fell behind, he'd be in trouble. "I'm looking to find a fastball and swing because it's hard enough coming off the bench cold trying to do something. It's even worse trying to see an off-speed pitch," Hamilton said. "That's the last thing a pinch hitter wants to see in a situation like that. It's one of those few times where I went up there thinking, 'If I see a fastball, I'm hacking.' I fouled off a couple of pitches and he got me with the splitter."

It was a testament to just how tough Clemens could be and precisely how dominant he was on that night. That was Clemens's ninth strikeout of the evening. Hamilton knew exactly what Clemens was going to do. He even got a fastball to hit, but he couldn't do anything with it. "That's the difference between a guy who's swinging the bat well and a guy who's not. You go up there looking for a certain pitch, you get that pitch, a guy who's going well puts it in play. He does something with it. A guy who's not, he fouls that pitch off or he misses it. In the big leagues you can't miss too many pitches. The pitching is so good, believe it or not, I know a lot of people don't think the pitching is that great in the big leagues now compared to years ago, but still, guys usually give you one pitch to hit and if you don't get that pitch, you're done."

Hamilton was done in that at bat. The Mets were finished off in Game 5 when the Yankees scored twice in the top of the ninth to capture their fourth World Series title in five years. Hamilton fought his way through one more season with the Mets before he was released in July of that year. He entered the world of broadcast journalism, serving as an on-air host for MLB.com's MLB Radio for years before taking a post with the commissioner's office in 2007. Officially, he's the senior specialist for on-field operations, assisting in the decision-making process for fines, suspensions, umpires, pace of play, that sort of thing. Hamilton feels he's in the perfect position for a former player who wanted to stay in the game.

He also could be in right spot to get some legitimate insight into what really happened back on October 22, 2000. He can imagine a scenario where he could just up and ask Clemens about what was going on in his mind, though it's not something that's occurred to him to do in the past. "If we were sitting at a table at three in the morning, drinks are flowing, no one is really in their right mind and you just bust out, 'What the hell were you thinking about?'" Hamilton suggested. "I've got friends of ours, we're in that same kind of group where it could happen. I've had ample opportunity to ask him, but I've never thought about it, to be honest with you."

LUIS **GONZALEZ** (2001)

IT WOULD BE EASY TO ASSUME that any game Roger Clemens started, he would be the clear focus of attention, especially games on larger stages like the World Series. While that sometimes was the case, Clemens was involved in some huge games in the Fall Classic that ended up being remembered for far more than the fact he took the mound.

If Exhibit A is Game 6 of the 1986 World Series, then Exhibit B would be Game 7 in the 2001 Series that pitted Clemens and the New York Yankees against the Arizona Diamondbacks, playing one of the better World Series in recent memory. Clemens pitched an exceptional game, but the Diamondback late-inning heroics, on the mound courtesy of Randy Johnson and at the plate by Luis Gonzalez, trumped Clemens's start much in the way Mookie Wilson and the Mets had fifteen years prior.

Before Gonzalez blooped the single off of Mariano Rivera that ended the Yankees run of World Series titles, he had gone 0 for 3 against Clemens in Game 7. Back in Game 3, a huge win for Clemens and the Yankees as they stared at a 0–2 deficit, Gonzalez had gone 1 for 3 against the Rocket. But their history pre-dated this World Series matchup.

When Luis Gonzalez reached the big leagues, it was with the Houston Astros in 1990. He established himself the following season and would spend seven full seasons in the National League. After filing for free agency following the 1997 season, he signed a deal with the Detroit Tigers, deciding to give the American League a whirl. It gave Gonzalez the chance to see a lot of things and opponents he hadn't been able to during his tenure in the senior circuit. Inter-league play had just finished its debut season in 1997, so the idea of seeing more of the other league was still in its infancy. Signing with the Tigers, Gonzalez thought, would broaden his horizons as a baseball player and allow him to travel to sights previously unseen and face some of the greater players from the other league he had only read about or seen on TV.

"Now, obviously, it's a lot different with inter-league play," Gonzalez said. "I got to play in different ballparks where I hadn't been before. I'd been in the National League primarily throughout my career until I had that crossover, going to the American League. Getting the chance to face one of the elite pitchers was something I was looking forward to as well."

Clemens was just coming off Year One of his Toronto renaissance, winning his fourth Cy Young Award in his first season with the Blue Jays. Gonzalez had just finished a one-year return engagement with the Astros after a turn with the Chicago Cubs. Gonzalez had always been a capable, if not spectacular, hitter. It wouldn't be for another year, when he went back to the National League and joined the Arizona Diamondbacks, that he would join the elite ranks of top-notch run producers. In 1998 the lefty-swinging outfielder did show some signs of prepping for that breakout. His lone season in the American League saw him set then-career highs in home runs (23), doubles (35), total bases (260) and slugging percentage (.475). He faced Clemens four times that season, going a combined 2 for 10 in the four games, all eventual Blue Jays wins.

Clemens was masterful in those four outings, not shocking considering how locked in he was and that the Tigers lost ninety-seven games in 1998. Clemens pitched a total of 31⅔ innings in those contests, allowing just 8 runs (2.27 ERA) and striking out 42. Gonzalez went 0 for his first 7 against Clemens, but that took nothing away from the experience of seeing what he could do against the best baseball had to offer at the time.

"I'd already been in Major League Baseball for six or seven years, then to go to the American League and have the opportunity to face a guy like that, who is a first-ballot Hall of Famer for sure, it's always a thrill," Gonzalez said. "It doesn't matter how many years you've played. When you get the opportunity to face a guy who has the reputation and the ability to be a strikeout artist and things like that, it's a challenge, especially for us as professional athletes to face somebody like that.

"As a hitter, you know he's one of the best out there. [Hitters] being offensive players, that's what you gear yourself for. You want to try and beat the best out there every single day. You take it as a challenge to go out there. You don't go out there intimidated, but at the same time, you know what kind of credentials the guy has. He's been around forever and he's got Hall of Fame numbers. Even back then, he was destined to be a first-ballot Hall of Famer."

That makes what happened on September 16, 1998, all the more special. In the third meeting of the season between the two teams, Clemens carried a two-hit shutout and 2–0 lead into the seventh inning when Gonzalez came to the plate with nary a hit in his nascent career against the Blue Jay ace. Maybe he learned something from the seven other outs he made or perhaps he just guessed right, but Gonzalez homered to lead off that inning for his first hit against Clemens, pulling the Tigers within a run (they'd go on to lose the game, 2–1). Interestingly, Gonzalez remembers more about the next time he faced Clemens, ten days later on September 26, than about the home run itself.

"I remember, either my next at bat or the one after, I got dusted," Gonzalez recalled. "He was one of those guys. He made his presence known out there on the mound and he didn't care who you were. A lot of pitchers thrive on intimidation, trying to not let hitters feel comfortable up there at the plate, and he was definitely one of those guys.

"It's a sign of respect but at the same time, you know he's got great control out there. He knows what he's doing with the ball. You take it in stride; you know it's part of the game and you know that's part of his repertoire. When he goes out there and pitches, he does things like that from time to time just like Pedro Martinez did and others have."

Gonzalez didn't have a chance to seek retribution for another three years, and when he did, it was on the biggest stage imaginable to him at the time. Gonzalez was a late bloomer of sorts and didn't attend his first All-Star Game until 1999, at age thirty-one and in his ninth full season in the big leagues. That season, he was a reserve outfielder for the National League after joining the Diamondbacks, replacing Larry Walker in the fourth inning. Two years later, in 2001, Gonzalez was chosen by fans to start the game, held in Seattle, the first and only time he was so honored.

Not only was he in the starting lineup, but he had the pleasure of playing out of position in center field and leading off the game. The first pitch came from a New York Yankee who was 12–1 with a 3.55 ERA and 122 strikeouts in 124⅓ IP. Roger Clemens was in his third season with the Yankees. He'd won World Series rings the previous two years and the team looked like they were headed for a third go-round. At the break, the Bronx Bombers were 52–34 en route to a ninety-five-win season and held a game and a half lead over the Red Sox. It had become a nearly annual occurrence that Joe Torre was the manager of the American League team come All-Star time and he rewarded his veteran pitcher with his second All-Star start.

"It was exciting for me. I was having a great year," said Gonzalez, who hit .325 with career highs in home runs (57), RBIs (142), and a host of other offensive categories. "To be the leadoff hitter in the game, in the All-Star Game, that was a thrill. And you're facing one of the best in baseball in Roger Clemens. It definitely was something that I'll never forget."

Not that his at bat against Clemens was all that memorable. He popped to third as the Rocket pitched two perfect innings for the American League. Gonzalez did single off of Yankee teammate and close Clemens friend Andy Pettitte in his second and final All-Star at bat, but that was a Midsummer Classic most remembered for Cal Ripken Jr.'s home run in his final appearance before retiring.

Even though Gonzalez didn't get to inflict much damage on Clemens in Seattle that July, even at the break it appeared that the two might get the chance to meet again in October. Gonzalez and the Diamondbacks were also in first place at the end of the first half, leading the NL West by 3½ games. They would end up winning the division by a couple of games over the San Francisco Giants.

The Diamondbacks's path to the World Series took them through St. Louis and Atlanta. It took Arizona all five games to get past the Cardinals in the National League Division Series, then just five more to dispatch the Braves in the best-of-seven National League Championship Series. The Yankees nearly didn't make it out of the American League Division Series to add this chapter to their rich World Series history. They trailed the Oakland A's 2–0 with the series moving to Oakland. But they managed to come back, capped off by the now famous "Jeter flip" play, and win the series in five. That gave them some serious momentum and they were able to defeat the Mariners in five games in the American League Championship Series to reach the World Series for the fourth consecutive season.

Clemens, who had finished the year 20–3 and took home Cy Young Award number five, started Games 1 and 5 of the ALDS and was uneven, at best. He yielded 9 hits and 5 runs in 8⅓ innings, losing Game 1 and getting a no-decision in Game 5. It was his second straight year of struggling in the ALDS against Oakland. He made two starts as well in 2000 and lost them both, finishing with an 8.18 ERA. In both instances he bounced back with a strong ALCS outing against the Mariners. In 2001 he went just five innings in Game 4, thanks to 4 walks, but gave up no runs in the process. It was a big start on the heels of a 14–3 thrashing by the Mariners in Game 3 and the Yankees finished off Seattle in the next game.

That set the stage for the World Series, and it turned out to be one of the greatest Fall Classics in memory. The series opened in Arizona, in what was then called Bank One Ballpark. The organization may have been new to the postseason, but fans at the BOB were fired up throughout the Series and certainly played a part in the Diamondbacks opening up with a 9–1 victory behind Curt Schilling. Randy Johnson followed suit with a 4–0 shutout to send the series to New York with the Yankees down two.

Clemens was again asked to play stopper and he came through one more time in Game 3 at Yankee Stadium. He got locked in a duel with lefty Brian Anderson, who pitched into the sixth and gave up just a couple of earned runs. Clemens was a notch better, going seven and allowing just 1 run on 3 hits while striking out 9. Mariano Rivera came in and threw two absolutely dominant innings to shut the door, something the Yankees were counting on happening again at the end of the series. Aside from the one at bat in the All-Star Game that July, Gonzalez hadn't faced the Rocket in three years. Clemens's evolution had continued and Gonzalez certainly noticed some differences in the then-thirty-nine-year-old.

"I think everyone changes. You change as years go by and you make adjustments," said Gonzalez, who went 1 for 3 against Clemens in Game 3. "What he's been able to do, he's been able to stay on top of his game with whatever changes he's made, with his work ethic and things like that. Guys like that live for that stage. They love being in the big spotlight and he doesn't disappoint when he's in there. He always steps up to the challenge.

"For us, we had a good ball club. We were facing one of the better staffs in baseball. At that time the Yankees were running their championship drives year in and year out. Fortunately, for us, we had two big horses on our team, too, by the names of Randy Johnson and Curt Schilling. We matched up just as well against those guys."

Games 4 and 5 were both extra-inning affairs. The Yankees won Game 4 thanks to a ninth-inning home run by Tino Martinez to tie it and a tenth-inning blast by Derek Jeter to send the Bronx into rapture. The Diamondbacks once again had a lead in Game 5, but for the second straight night Byung-

Hyun Kim gave up a two-run home run in the ninth—this time to Scott Brosius—that kept them from taking a commanding series lead. Manager Bob Brenly's decision to bring in Kim again led to some of the greatest second-guessing in World Series history. The Yankees ended up winning that one in the twelfth on an Alfonso Soriano RBI single that gave them a 3–2 lead. The Series headed back to Arizona with New York needing only one win in two tries for a four-peat.

Game 6 was over before it started. Andy Pettitte got knocked out in the third and the Diamondbacks had scored 15 runs through four innings, allowing everyone to look ahead early to the one-game, winner-takes-all Game 7 the following night. Randy Johnson went seven relatively pressure-free innings thanks to the run support, something that would prove to be crucial the next day.

Often in a Game 7, with two aces on the mound, the contest doesn't live up to the hype. This Game 7, with Clemens facing Schilling, more than made up for past disappointments. Both right-handers put up zeroes through five innings before the Diamondbacks were able to string a pair of hits together in the sixth to take a 1–0 lead. It didn't last long as the Yankees responded in kind to tie the game in the top of the seventh. Clemens came out to start the bottom of the inning, but after striking out Schilling and giving up a Tony Womack single, the game was handed over to the Yankees vaunted bullpen.

"You know there's not going to be a lot of offense when there's a guy like that out there, so you have to scratch and claw and try to get every opportunity you can to try and score runs," said Gonzalez, who went a combined 1 for 5 in the two Clemens World Series starts. "There's not really frustration but you have to know that if there's an opportunity to draw a walk or move a guy over, you can't miss out on those opportunities. You have to try to take advantage of them because you don't get them too often. They don't give in very easily. You just have to try and manufacture anyway you can off of those guys."

They managed to manufacture just the one and Clemens left with a 10-strikeout performance then had to watch as the drama unfolded. And much like 1986, what happened in those final innings in many ways overshadowed what Clemens accomplished that night. Soriano homered to lead off the eighth inning to give the Yankees a 2–1 lead. Closer extraordinaire Mariano Rivera, he of the microscopic career postseason ERA, was up and loosening before Soriano's ball hit the ground. Those who had seen past World Series and what Rivera had done to the Diamondbacks up to that point—five scoreless, virtually unhittable innings—thought the Series was all but over. After Rivera struck out the side in the eighth, Gonzalez being the first victim that inning, members of the media started lining up outside the Yankees clubhouse in anticipation of covering one more New York title.

The Diamondbacks, of course, had other ideas. Not that they were happy to see Rivera enter the game, but they may have been somewhat relieved that Clemens was no longer on the mound. In 13⅓

World Series innings that fall, Clemens finished with a 1.35 ERA, yielding 10 hits and striking out 19.

"You were hoping he'd get tired. He was throwing so well," Gonzalez said. "They get amped up for games like that and they feed off of the adrenaline and the juices from the fans and it being Game 7 of the World Series. He was definitely on his game that night and fortunately for us, we were able to get a couple of hits off of their relievers and score some runs to win Game 7.

"You were trying to get a run anyway you can. It's the World Series, he was on his game, just as Curt was on his game that night. We brought in Randy to relieve and they brought in Mariano to close out the game. We were fortunate enough to get a couple of hits there to take it away from those guys."

Right before Rivera came in, presumably to shut the door, Randy Johnson entered in the eighth to relieve for the Diamondbacks. This was the same Randy Johnson who had pitched seven innings the night before. He came in to face the lefty Paul O'Neill, who was lifted for pinch hitter Chuck Knoblauch. The Big Unit, who beat Schilling for NL Cy Young honors in both 2001 and 2002, got Knoblauch to fly out, and most would have accepted that Johnson was being used just for that one batter. But he wasn't. When Johnson pitched a perfect ninth, striking out Jorge Posada to end the frame, it undoubtedly sent electricity through the crowd at the BOB.

"I don't think there was any surprise," Gonzalez said about Johnson coming into the game. "Once you get in those games, pitchers volunteer and players

volunteer. You don't know if you're going to get another opportunity like that. You have all off-season
to rest, so everybody's available, everybody's doing
whatever they can to help their team win. It's all
about winning that ring. You realize it's not as easy as
it looks to go out there and win a championship, so
you try to do everything you can to take advantage of
that opportunity whenever you can."

The Diamondbacks took advantage of a leadoff
single by Mark Grace in the bottom of the ninth. A
Rivera error on a bunt was also welcomed with open
arms. A Tony Womack double tied the score and then
it was Gonzalez who got to play hero, blooping a single
just over the drawn-in Yankees infield into center field
to give the Diamondbacks the unexpected Series win.

"It definitely was a lot of fun," Gonzalez said, a
slight understatement. "Good pitching matchups,
good defense, and timely hitting on both sides. It was
my first Fall Classic and it's definitely one I'll never
forget because they were all nail-biters all the way
through. The blowout game was in Game 6 when we
jumped on Pettitte early, but aside from that... The
way the World Series turned out, the home team won
every single game."

As Gonzalez pointed out, as much as his timely
hit won the Series, it was the tandem of Johnson and
Schilling that was responsible for edging Clemens and
company. It's far less daunting to dig in against Roger
Clemens when he's on his game when you know
you've got a pair of guys who can be just as, if not
more, dominant. Schilling and Johnson shared Series
MVP honors and their numbers for the seven-game

nail-biter almost dwarf Clemens's outstanding performance. Schilling started three games, earning one victory. In his 21⅓ innings of work, he gave up 4 runs (1.69 ERA), 12 hits, and only 2 walks while striking out 26. Johnson made two starts and the one relief appearance, recording 3 victories while allowing just 9 hits and 2 earned runs (1.05 ERA) and striking out 19 in 17⅓ innings pitched.

When Clemens made the switch over to the National League and joined the team—the Houston Astros—where Gonzalez began his career, the two were able to do battle a few more times. It was another three-season layoff between at bats, but Gonzalez had his best day against Clemens the first time they met in July 2004. The outfielder went 2 for 3 for his only multi-hit game against the Rocket. In two 2005 matchups, Gonzalez managed to go just 1 for 6 with a pair of strikeouts. Two more games in 2006 provided no help. Gonzalez went 0 for 6 in those two games against Clemens, to bring his regular-season line against the future Hall of Famer to 5 for 27, which translates to a less-than-stellar, but fairly typical against this pitcher, .185 average. Adding in his World Series 1 for 5 actually helps the average climb to .188. There is a way to approach a pitcher like Clemens, according to Gonzalez. It's just one of those easier-said-than-done things.

"You try to get him early, because he came up with the splitter and things like that and it made it that much tougher," Gonzalez said. "Not only that, when you have a pitcher like that, you don't want to get deep into the count because he is a strikeout-type pitcher, so you try to get that guy early, get something up in the zone, and try to get a good pass at it.

"With him, what made it so effective is that he threw so hard, his fastball, everybody gears up for his fastball and a lot of times guys were almost guessing he was going to throw the fastball, and then when he threw the splitter, they were so far out in front, it made your swing looked so bad. A guy throwing 96–97 miles per hour doesn't give you a lot of time to think up there. You just have to go up there and react."

Even though their careers as established major leaguers have run concurrently for seventeen years, their paths did not cross all too often on the field. Gonzalez may not have seen Clemens enough to learn how to go up and react to find success at the plate. Few hitters have. But Gonzalez has managed to crack the Clemens inner sanctum, becoming a rare opponent who can consider Clemens a friend. Their relationship, it turns out, came as a result of both calling Houston home during off-seasons for many years. The Clemens not between the lines, it seems, is quite a different animal than the one who's taken the ball every fifth day for the past twenty-five years. "I'm friends with him because I lived in Houston when he was there," Gonzalez said. "It was just nice to see him around. He's a great family guy. He likes having his boys around. They're all big now."

It's a side of Clemens few saw for most of his career. When he returned to Houston to play, however, word spread of a kinder, gentler Clemens. It clearly never impacted his competitive nature on the field, but perhaps being home during the season allowed him to have the off-season Roger meet the in-season Roger halfway. "He's different. He's a little bit more open [off the field]," Gonzalez said. "The last couple of years with Houston, there were a lot of young guys there, I think that opened him up a little bit more around his teammates. I never played with him during the season, but I know a lot of guys who have played with him there in Houston and they all said he was great, a fantastic guy to be around.

"What he does now so well is he helps a lot of these young kids. He spent time in the Houston Astros organization going around talking to some of these younger players. And that means a lot to those young kids."

As much as Clemens's words have an impact on the up-and-comers, Clemens has always seemed like a lead-by-example type. It's been an easy example to follow. Work harder than anyone else. That, plus a super-healthy dose of God-given talent, can give you a Hall of Fame career. In all seriousness, Clemens's drive is as much, if not more, responsible for what he has accomplished than his ability to throw a fastball in the upper 90s.

"He loves competing," Gonzalez said. "That drive inside of him is what keeps him going. The guy has always had a great work ethic and he's continued to dominate at this day and age. You don't see that very often and that's why he's one of the elite athletes that have ever played this game."

Knowing this about his neighbor enabled Gonzalez to take the news that Clemens was returning for at least one more go-round in 2007 with the New York Yankees fairly easily. He was neither shocked nor floored. If anything, Gonzalez just had to smile when he found out the Rocket would be on the mound one more time. Even if the two never meet again—it only would have happened if the Yankees and Dodgers made it to the World Series—Gonzalez realizes having Clemens out there every fifth day is simply good for the game of baseball.

"I'm not surprised [he came back]," Gonzalez said. "There's a need for guys like that. He's one of those guys who's in demand, so he keeps running out there and pitching."

JUAN **PIERRE** (2003)

ROGER CLEMENS WALKED OFF the mound at Pro Player Stadium in Miami on October 22, 2003, after striking out Luis Castillo to end the seventh inning. With his spot due to lead off the eighth, he and the nearly 66,000 fans on hand knew he would be lifted for a pinch hitter.

After all, it was Game 4 of the World Series and the home team, the Marlins, had a 3–1 lead in the game, though they were trailing 2–1 in the Series at the time. Normally, a visiting pitcher finished a start without much notice. But this wasn't just any ordinary start. From the opening pitch witnesses sensed it was something different. Everyone thought this was the last start in Roger Clemens's illustrious career. Fans in the stands and Marlins in the dugout stood and applauded Clemens as he left the field, creating one of the best feel-good moments in World Series history.

That is, of course, until Clemens decided the next year to come back and pitch for the Houston Astros.

"He ruined it all," said Juan Pierre, the Marlins leadoff hitter that season. "That was something you were going to be able to tell your grandkids, that you saw Roger Clemens's last pitch and it was in the

World Series. He came back and ruined that story. Now it looks like he's never going to stop pitching. It was definitely one of the better moments of the World Series and of my career.

"I think the fans kind of brought everybody else into it. You kind of realized the significance of it. At the time you thought that would be the last pitch you'd see from him. It was just respecting what he's done in the game, his longevity, and his ability to be good for so long. I think the crowd started it and everyone else took hold of it after that just to show respect and honor for him."

Clemens had gone seven strong innings in the game, allowing 3 runs on 8 hits while striking out 5. But that only tells part of the story. The Marlins got to him for 3 runs in the first inning, picking up 5 of those hits. One of them was a two-run homer from Miguel Cabrera. Then Clemens shut the door for the next six frames, giving the visiting Yankees the chance to come back. They didn't do so until the ninth, when Ruben Sierra's two-run triple knotted the score. Marlins shortstop Alex Gonzalez ended up playing unlikely hero, hitting a walk-off homer to lead off the twelfth inning and tie the Series at two games apiece.

"He was the aggressor he usually is," said Pierre, who went 0 for 4 against Clemens that night. "He'll try to intimidate you. He had just as good stuff. He had all of his pitches working that night. It's a big testament to Miguel Cabrera because [Clemens] came up and in, like he usually does, then he ended up hitting Roger out opposite field. That was a big, big thing in our game, realizing we could get him. We could hit him."

When they could see him. Especially when Pierre led off the game and when Clemens retired his final batter, there were some external distractions from the stands. It seemed like there were 60,000 amateur photographers trying to capture the historical moments. "Poor Luis Castillo, he was the last batter he faced," Pierre recalled. "He was trying to hit in a strobe light because all the flashes were going off every pitch."

Not only did the constant flashing create a distraction, it also served as a reminder of just how big a deal this was. As if playing in the World Series wasn't enough, the Marlins had to deal with a legend supposedly on his way out. The Marlins had stolen Game 1 in New York, with Pierre leading the way. The leadoff man, who had played every regular-season game in 2003, hit .305 and led the National League with 65 steals, had gone 2 for 3 with 2 RBIs, a walk, and a stolen base in his first World Series contest. The Yankees bounced back in Game 2 behind a strong outing from Andy Pettitte to send the series to Florida tied at one. Now it was the Marlins who had the home-field advantage.

It wouldn't last long. The Yankees turned things back in their favor with a 6–1 victory in Game 3, with Mike Mussina going seven strong innings for the win. That set the stage for Clemens to take the mound in Game 4 and a chance to give the Yankees a commanding 3–1 series lead. He had provided a huge lift in Game 3 of the American League Division Series that fall, beating the Minnesota Twins at their place to give the Yankees a 2–1 series lead. They finished off the series by crushing Minnesota, 8–1, in Game 4.

He was a little more uneven in the ALCS against the Boston Red Sox. He did win Game 3 by allowing 2 runs over six innings, once again giving the Yankees a 2–1 edge in the series. He was not so effective in the deciding Game 7. He pitched only into the fourth inning, allowing 4 runs (3 earned) on 6 hits. When he departed with none out in that fourth inning, Boston was up 4–0 with Pedro Martinez on the mound. But New York found a way to claw back and tie the game before Aaron Boone sent the Yankees to the World Series with a walk-off homer leading off the eleventh inning.

That momentum did not carry over into the World Series with the Marlins taking Game 1, though by the time Clemens took the mound again for Game 4—six days after the ALCS Game 7 start—it was the Yankees looking to take command of the Series. Reflecting on the game now, Pierre realizes how special it was to face that kind of pitcher on that stage. At the time, though, that couldn't enter his thoughts. There was no room to be in awe of a legend saying farewell to the sport when there was a championship to be won.

"It was tough, the first pitch he threw of the night, there were so many cameras going off and things like that," Pierre said. "I tried to set the emotions aside and just play the game. Maybe if it was a regular-season game, it'd be different, but it was a World Series game. We knew Roger was out there, but we were trying to win the World Series. If it were a regular-season game, you would've been, 'Man, this is Roger Clemens's last time.' But in the World Series, that kind of overshadowed him for me."

For many of the Marlins that autumn, it was the
first time they had dug in against Clemens. It was the
kind of situation Clemens thrived on throughout his
career, using his aura and intimidating presence to
unsettle hitters, especially younger ones. That made
Florida's ability to put three runs on the board right
out of the gate even more impressive. They may have
been in awe, but they were not overwhelmed. Pierre,
for his part, had faced Clemens once before. The center fielder spent two and one-half seasons with the
Colorado Rockies before being traded to Florida
following the 2002 season. In that campaign the Yankees visited Coors Field in Colorado for an interleague series. On June 20, Clemens and company got
to see what the friendly confines in Denver were all
about.

Clemens went just four innings in the contest,
pitching to two batters in the fifth before departing.
Clemens gave up a couple of runs in the contest,
which turned into a Coors Field 14–11, ten-inning
slugfest won by the Rockies on Todd Zeile's walk-off,
three-run homer.

Pierre singled off of Clemens to lead things off,
but he was promptly picked off. It was his single in
the fifth that chased Clemens from the game. Pierre
ended up with a 4 for 6 showing in the game. It was
the start of a fairly successful run for Pierre against
Clemens in the next several years.

In that 2003 World Series, however, Clemens had
Pierre's number in Game 4. Though Clemens was ef-
fective, it was another young gun from the Lone Star
State who stole the show in that Fall Classic.

Josh Beckett was born eighteen years after Roger Clemens. Like Clemens, he's a hard-throwing right-hander who was a first-round draft pick, only he heard his name called by the Marlins sixteen years after Clemens was selected by the Red Sox, and he came out of the high school, not college, ranks. But as Beckett and countless other right-handers from Texas have found out, if you're a hard thrower from that state, you're almost automatically going to be compared to Roger Clemens or Nolan Ryan. And it should come as no surprise that those from succeeding generations of Texan pitchers look up to the Rocket and the Express.

It seemed like the stars were aligned in the fall of 2003. With Clemens supposedly riding off into the sunset, there was a perfect opportunity for the new generation to take the helm. Beckett heard it knock and he answered the door with a huge postseason performance. Then twenty-three years old, he pitched well in his NLDS start against the Giants. He appeared in three games in the NLCS against the Cubs, tossing a complete-game shutout in Game 5, then coming back for four innings of effective relief in Game 7.

But he was just getting started. He got the loss in Game 3 of the World Series, but to call him a tough-luck loser would be an understatement. He gave up just 3 hits and 2 runs in 7⅓ innings against the Yankees, striking out 10 along the way. It just happened that Mike Mussina was a touch better that night.

Beckett saved the best for last. The Marlins led the Series, 3–2, with all of the momentum as they headed back to New York. Florida had won Games 4 and 5, including that thrilling twelfth-inning victory in the game Clemens had started. The Marlins needed to win just one of the two final games to capture the franchise's second World Series title. Beckett decided to end the drama in Game 6. He tossed his second complete-game shutout of the postseason, giving up 5 hits and striking out 9 on his way to earning World Series MVP honors. There was no official ceremony, but it certainly seemed like there was a changing of the guard at Yankee Stadium that night.

"We had a couple of flamethrowers like that, with Brad Penny being similar," Pierre said. "But Beckett, being from Texas, grew up idolizing Roger Clemens. He was growing into his own. The performance he had in Game 6, it was Roger Clemens–like. It looked like the torch was being passed. As we know now, though, Roger is still carrying the torch."

Pierre and the Marlins got to see that the torch was still burning quite brightly in 2004, Clemens's first with the Houston Astros. Clemens went seven innings for the victory against Florida on May 11, striking out 11 Marlins and allowing just a run, his seventh straight win to start the 2004 season. Pierre went 0 for 3 against Clemens, though he did collect a single against reliever Brad Lidge after Clemens had departed the game.

The 2005 season would be Pierre's last with the Marlins. Florida conducted a major fire sale after the season, sending Pierre to the Cubs for a trio of young pitchers. He did have the chance to face Clemens wearing the Marlins teal twice more before the deal.

Both were Clemens victories, with the Rocket allowing just a run in 13⅓ innings, yielding 9 hits and
striking out 10 in the process. The first of his two
wins was victory number 330, moving him past Steve
Carlton into ninth place on the all-time list. Pierre
went 2 for 7 in the two games and saw a pitcher who
wasn't throwing quite as hard as he did back in the
World Series. That didn't mean, though, he was any
less effective on the mound.

"He just threw a lot more off-speed stuff to me,"
Pierre said. "But he still was the same because he
pitched inside. He had a lot of sink in his ball; his ball
sunk a lot more with the two-seamer, but he was still
the same aggressor. He still had the intimidation factor when he stood on the mound. He was pretty
much the same. I never faced him back, back in the
day when he was like 96–97, but he was still around
92–93, but the sink was the big thing."

The 2006 season saw Pierre land with his third
team. The Marlins had gone 83–79 for the second
straight season in 2005. That put Florida in third
place in the National League East in both seasons.
Marlins ownership had made a series of moves to
maintain a winning ballclub without success. First
baseman Derrek Lee was dealt after the 2003 season
before he started making serious money. At the same
time, Ivan Rodriguez, who had inked a one-year deal,
signed a free-agent contract with the Detroit Tigers
after helping the Marlins win their ring.

At the trading deadline in 2004, they traded for
catcher Paul LoDuca, sending Brad Penny to the
Dodgers in that deal. Prior to the 2005 season, they

inked first baseman Carlos Delgado to a big free-agent contract and brought back veteran left-hander Al Leiter, jettisoned the last time the franchise had a fire sale following the 1997 season, to help the rotation.

Then Florida decided these moves weren't going to work and it was time to pare down payroll to the bare minimum again. Granted, it was different ownership, with Jeffrey Loria at the helm instead of Wayne Hyzinga, but the results were the same. Leiter was the first to go, on July 16, 2005, as part of a conditional deal with the Yankees.

During that off-season, the ship was really blown up. LoDuca and Delgado were shipped to the Mets in separate deals that brought in a slew of pitching prospects. Beckett and third baseman Mike Lowell headed to Boston for a boatload of minor leaguers, including future NL Rookie of the Year Hanley Ramirez. Even lifelong Marlin Luis Castillo, one of the few who were around for both championships, was shipped off to Minnesota for a pair of minor leaguers.

Pierre was traded to the Chicago Cubs on December 7, 2005, for a trio of young pitchers, all of whom, to the Marlins decision maker's credit, have pitched in the big leagues for Florida. In 2006 he had another typical Juan Pierre year in many respects, hitting .292 and finishing second in the league in stolen bases for the third consecutive season. A strong second half helped the overall numbers look good, though his season was seen as a disappointment in Wrigleyland and he was allowed to play the free-agent market, landing with the Dodgers in 2007 courtesy of a five-year, $45 million contract.

Before that happened he did get the opportunity to play within the same division as Clemens for a season. Well, half a season, since Clemens didn't make his debut that year until June 22. The Cubs saw Clemens for his third start, at Minute Maid Park on July 3. It turned out to be Clemens's first victory of the season, though he went just five innings and allowed a pair of runs. The Cubs were already well out of the race by then, twenty-one games under .500. The Astros were also under .500, but they were just five games behind the St. Louis Cardinals. The victory pulled them to within four games. Pierre tried to do his part, despite having hit just .255 over the season's first three months. The center fielder went 2 for 3 with a double and triple, though neither extra-base hit resulted in a run.

It marked the beginning of Pierre's best month with the Cubs. He hit .345 in July of 2006 to help fuel a .311 second-half performance. He got another crack at Clemens later in the month, on July 19. And this turned out to be more than just a regular-season game when put into historical context.

Clemens's mound opponent was fellow right-hander Greg Maddux, himself a 300-game winner. The two had met a year earlier in an even more highly anticipated "matchup for the ages." Before the two faced each other in that game—won by Maddux, 3–2— two 300-game winners had not met since 1987 when Steve Carlton was finishing his career with the Minnesota Twins and Don Sutton was in his twilight with the California Angels. To find the last similar contest in the National League prior to Clemens-Maddux I, you'd have to go all the way back to 1892 when Philadelphia's Tim Keefe and St. Louis's Jim "Pud" Galvin went toe-to-toe.

Needless to say, Clemens-Maddux II got nearly as much attention as their first meeting, especially with Wrigley Field as the appropriately historic backdrop. This time it was Clemens emerging victorious, 3–2. It was win number 343, moving him into sole possession of eighth place on the career victories list. The Rocket tossed six shutout innings on the night, as he approached his forty-fourth birthday. Maddux, forty at the time, gave up 3 runs in seven innings of work. Pierre went 1 for 3 on the night and it was when he got that one base hit that Clemens showed he still had the higher-octane stuff to turn to when it was needed.

It was the sixth inning, Clemens's final frame. Pierre led off with a single and promptly stole second to give the Cubs only their second runner in scoring position that night. It was a hot, muggy night in Chicago and Clemens hadn't been lighting up the radar gun at all, showing he could still be effective without the plus fastball he had in years past. But with Pierre on second and the dangerous Derrek Lee up, Clemens reached back and threw a 91-mile-per-hour fastball by Lee for the second out of the inning before inducing a ground ball from Aramis Ramirez to finish his outing unscathed. "I remember that, they hyped that up pretty well, with two 300-game winners on the mound," Pierre said. "It was at Wrigley Field. You can get caught up in the moment.

"Every time I've faced him, he's been pretty much as good as advertised. He throws a lot of strikes; he pounds the strike zone. There's not too much drop-off, from 2003 to now. It's amazing a guy that age continues to throw the ball like he does, as hard as he does. That's the most remarkable thing. He still has the velocity. He may not have the 95, but he's got 92 with good movement. He's got the cutter now, a sinker, a slider. He's mixing it up, learning how to pitch even more now that his velocity has dropped. He's not afraid to move your feet. As a hitter you never like guys who'll move your feet. And he'll definitely do that if you get too comfortable."

No one was comfortable on August 15, 2006. The Cubs and Astros played an eighteen-inning marathon that night, with Chicago winning, scoring twice in the top of the eighteenth, at Minute Maid Park in Houston. The Astros were barely clinging to playoff hopes, 6½ games back of St. Louis and 4 back in the wild card, with several teams in front of them. It wasn't until a late-September run and Cardinals fade that Houston truly snuck into the picture, but as of this final meeting between Clemens and the Cubs they were close enough to merely gaze longingly at a playoff spot.

Pierre ended up having eight at bats in the game, but he led it off with a triple off Clemens, who pitched six uneven innings that saw him yield 5 runs on 7 hits. Pierre scored the first of those runs in that opening frame. He went 1 for 4 against Clemens, striking out to end the sixth inning in what could be the last time the speedy outfielder ever faces the Rocket. A strikeout normally wouldn't garner much attention against a guy who's second on the all-time K list. But this one is worth mentioning. In twenty-three career at bats against Roger Clemens, it was the only time Pierre ever carried the bat back to the dugout.

"I just don't swing the bat hard enough," Pierre said, half jokingly. "My no-strike swing is the same as my two-strike swing, almost. I guess I have the ability to put the ball in play. I'm not saying I got lucky, but you have to put good swings on good pitches because he doesn't make too many mistakes. I don't swing that hard. I won't say it's easier for me to make contact, but the fact that I [am a contact hitter] may have helped.

"You're aware of a guy when he gets two strikes, he's struck out so many guys, he knows how to put guys away. My whole thing is not letting him get to those two strikes a lot."

It's a philosophy many hitters have taken to heart when facing Clemens: Try to get him early in the count because if you fall behind, you're going to be in trouble more often than not. "You never like to go two strikes, especially against a guy like Roger Clemens," Pierre said. "I don't necessarily swing at the first pitch, but I definitely don't want to go deep in the count. The deeper in the count you go with Roger Clemens, you do get into his arsenal a little more. He can throw the splitty down and away, the slider and the curve in on your hands. It's safe to say you do want to get him early in the count before he can get into all those pitches. Typically, when I've had some success, I've hit off the first two or three pitches he's thrown."

Typically, that's what Pierre has done against all pitchers he's faced throughout his career. He's always among the league leaders in fewest pitches seen per at bat. In many ways he's been miscast as a leadoff hitter because of his speed. With a career batting average over .300 giving him a seemingly acceptable on-base percentage, that's masked somewhat, but if he doesn't get a base hit—and usually early in the count—he doesn't normally get on. That's why his EqA (equivalent average), a sabermetric measure of total offensive value per out, is just .256. His approach consistently has been swing early and often.

"It all depends on the pitcher," Pierre countered. "Some pitchers it doesn't matter if you see five pitches from the dugout, the guy's nasty, so you better try and get on base and score the run to make things happen. Typically, you do want to see a lot of pitches. But with Roger Clemens, you counter that with getting on base. If you can get on, steal a base, and try to do those things, that will take away his nastiness when there's a guy on base."

In many ways Pierre's line against Clemens is a microcosm of his entire career. He's struck out just once, right in line with what he does against all pitchers. Pierre is the active career leader in at bats per strikeout, a stat he's led the National League in every year of his career except one, and he finished sixth that season. Over the course of his career, he goes more than sixteen and a half at bats before striking out, more than two at bats better than the next closest player on the career active list.

Conversely, he doesn't walk a whole heck of a lot and he's led the league in outs on multiple occasions. His career high in walks was fifty-five back in that

World Series year with Florida and he received just fifty-five free passes in 2006 and 2007 combined. So it should come as no surprise that there's a big zero in the BB column on his career stat sheet against Clemens.

At the same time, though, all that contact does lead to base hits. He's led the National League in hits twice and has finished in the top five three other times. And in those 23 at bats against Clemens, he has managed to pick up 8 hits for an impressive .348 batting average. He's got a double and two triples among those hits, giving him a much-higher-than-normal .565 slugging percentage against the Rocket, 200 points or so higher than his career SLG. "It's one of those things, I've taken a couple of good swings against him, but there's no rhyme or reason. I just get in there and try to do what I do against any other pitcher."

Roger Clemens is not "any other pitcher," obviously. Pierre may never have faced him when he was blowing letter-high smoke by people with regularity, but he understands how Clemens has evolved from that thrower to the pitcher he was when the center fielder saw him in the National League. It used to be that seeing pitches up in the zone from him, back in his Red Sox days especially, meant lights out for the hitter. Now, that's the only place you have a prayer of hitting him, though Pierre realizes it's a faint prayer more often than not.

"You try to make him get the ball up because he's throwing a lot more sinkers and two-seamers these days and not running the high fastball as much," Pierre offered before adding, as if it was a warning, "though he can still throw it when he needs it."

PURE DOMINATION

PHIL BRADLEY

THE DEFINITION OF PERFECTION for a pitcher tends to be very straightforward. No hits, no runs, no base runners: That's a perfect game.

Anyone who was at Fenway Park on April 29, 1986, however, might want to challenge that definition. Roger Clemens took the mound that night against the Seattle Mariners and proceeded to mow down batters like no one ever had in the history of the game. When it was all over and done with, Clemens had set a new record with 20 strikeouts, breaking the mark previously set by Hall of Famers Steve Carlton, Tom Seaver, and Nolan Ryan.

What's more amazing is that while he was sending twenty Mariners back to the dugout, he wasn't sending any of them to first base courtesy of a free pass. That's right, Clemens didn't walk a single batter. Unfortunately, almost no one was there to see it. Only 13,414 faithful showed up to Yawkey Way that cold spring evening. The Red Sox that night were an afterthought in Beantown. Football may have been on the minds of New England's fans right after the NFL draft that afternoon. (It was, after all, not that long after the Patriots had lost to the Chicago Bears in the Super Bowl.) At the same time the Boston Celtics were hosting the Atlanta Hawks in a second-round playoff game at Boston Garden.

It wasn't just fans who weren't interested in baseball on that Tuesday. Red Sox games typically were on WRKO-AM, but they had been pushed to WPLM on the FM side so that the Celtics, who would go on to win the NBA title that season, could be broadcast on WRKO. For most of the game, Jerry Buckley, the official team photographer, was the only guy with a camera in the camera well. The Boston Globe had just one writer staffing the game.

It wasn't only the Celtics, Patriots, and the climate taking the spotlight away. The Red Sox had finished a pedestrian 81–81 the previous year and this was just the eighteenth game of the season. They hadn't gone to the playoffs since 1975 and they were facing a Mariners team that was already 7–12, had never had a winning season, and was coming off back-to-back eighty-eight-loss seasons during which they hit .258 and .255. It was hard to get the motors revving for this matchup.

Then there was the Clemens factor. The twenty-three-year-old would quickly become a draw for years at Fenway, but in early 1986 he was still a bit of an unknown quantity. Sure, he had impressed in his debut season of 1984 and finished sixth in Rookie of the Year voting, even though he didn't come up until mid-May. He had a respectable 3.29 ERA in 1985, but he made just fifteen starts and was shut down in August because of a shoulder injury that required surgery. When he took the mound against the Mariners, it was just his fourth post-surgery start. In his previous three starts, he had gone 8⅔ innings in one, completed a second, and struck out 10 in the third. He was beginning to show he was fine, but he likely didn't truly convince anyone until the Mariners game that this would be a special season, one in which he would start the All-Star Game and go on to win both the Cy Young and MVP Awards.

And it wasn't even supposed to happen that night. Clemens had been slated to pitch in Kansas City on the previous Sunday, but the game had been canceled because of inclement weather. With an off day for travel on that Monday, Clemens approached Tuesday's start with six days rest. The extra time off didn't seem to bother him any. Clemens struck out the side to open the game, an early sign that perhaps the Rocket had his "A" game that night. Phil Bradley was the number-two hitter in the M's lineup that night and he was strikeout number 2 after Spike Owen led off the game with a whiff. Bradley was also K numbers 7, 15, and the record-breaking 20.

"The velocity was well in excess of above average," said Bradley, who played his last game in the big leagues in 1990. "Back then, we didn't play with radar guns and pitch counts and all that stuff. But you could tell just by the reaction to his fastball that we were going to be in for a long night."

With all of the buzz around the twenty strikeouts, the factor that lifted Clemens's feat above the heroics of Carlton, Seaver, and Ryan was forgotten. Amazingly, while he was making hitter after hitter miss, he was not missing at all. The Mariners were only able to put ten balls in play all night, and Clemens was certainly not hurting himself. Somewhat astoundingly, the right-hander did not walk a single batter (a feat he would duplicate in his second 20-K game a decade later). Carlton, Seaver, and Ryan, while not exactly wild, had walked a pair of batters each.

"You're going to strike out twenty guys, throwing as hard as he did," Bradley recalled with admiration. "Now, granted, I know I struck out on some balls and there probably were some other guys [who did as well], but the fact that he didn't walk anybody, that's phenomenal in its own right.

"He was a control power pitcher. He was a four-pitch pitcher, with a fastball, curveball, slider, and changeup. He had velocity, he had four pitches and he could truly throw all four for strikes. He wasn't a trick pitcher. Nowadays, you watch Roger Clemens pitch, a lot of times you'd have to say his out pitch is the split-finger. Back twenty years ago, his out pitch was basically any pitch he wanted to throw you. Every time you faced him, every at bat, if he'd get two strikes on you, he could throw any pitch he wanted to get you out."

That he was getting all the outs via the strikeout shouldn't be all that surprising once the Mariners lineup is more closely examined. Frankly, Seattle's hitters in 1986 created more wind than a tropical storm. They went on to strike out 1,148 times over the course of the season, then an American League record. (That dubious record was broken by the Detroit Tigers, who whiffed 1,268 times in 1996. Twenty of those strikeouts, not surprisingly, came at the hands of one Mr. Roger Clemens in one game. The Tampa

Bay Devil Rays took ownership of the honor by striking out 1,324 times in 2007.)

"If you go back and look over the ten games
around that game, I think we averaged over ten strikeouts a game," Bradley said. "We were out in Oakland
and they were striking us out ten times a game. We
had a team that struck out a lot. That's not to take
away from the way Clemens threw that night."

Bradley's memory serves him right. The Mariners
racked up 47 Ks in the four games before the Clemens
record, then followed that up with a 16-strikeout performance against Red Sox lefty Bruce Hurst and two
relievers. That's 83 strikeouts in a six-game span, an
average of 13.8 K's per game. Obviously, Bradley
wasn't the only one with a penchant for swinging and
missing, though the outfielder did strike out 134
times in 1986. Jim Presley struck out 172 times; Danny
Tartabull whiffed 157 times; Gorman Thomas, in his
final year before retiring, would go down on strikes
for Seattle 55 times in fifty-seven games before heading back to Milwaukee to K 50 more times in forty-
four games; Dave Henderson did it 95 times in 103
games and, somewhat ironically, would get traded to
the Red Sox in time to be a 1986 postseason hero for
Boston. By late April the entire team was averaging
9.2 strikeouts per game. All of this may make it seem
that the Mariners were sitting ducks for history to
drop in on them. The way Clemens was dealing,
though, even the stingiest of offenses could have
ended up where Seattle's did.

"It's easy, twenty-one years later, to say he
could've done it to anybody. But he could've done it

to anybody that night," said Bradley, who had struck out 20 times in a span of forty-four at bats that included the Clemens game. "It was a perfect combination of a team that strikes out a lot against a guy who was really on his game. The stars had to be aligned and they were aligned perfectly that night."

Over time the strikeout has always carried with it a negative connotation, more so than the average out. It's worse, some would say, because nothing good can come of it. If you put the ball in play, there's at least the chance of something good happening. While that might be true, some of the 1986 Mariners did have otherwise productive seasons. Presley hit 27 homers and drove in 107 runs, the only time in his career he topped the century mark in RBIs. Tartabull had 25 homers and 96 RBIs despite finishing fifth in the AL in strikeouts, one spot behind Presley. Bradley hit .310, finishing with a .405 OBP thanks to 77 walks, and stole 21 bases.

Bradley did not come up as a big strikeout kind of hitter. The Mariners third-round draft pick in 1981, he was a speedster who could hit for average and get on base. In his three seasons before making it to the big leagues, Bradley hit .322 with just 3 home runs and 114 stolen bases, 58 of them coming in 1982. His on-base percentage was always way over .400, and in 1983 he drew 73 walks against just 41 strikeouts. His first full year in the big leagues, 1984, saw more of the same. Bradley hit .301 as a rookie with nary a home run to be found, though he swiped 21 bags and had a very respectable .373 OBP.

Then 1985 happened. Bradley again hit .300 and stole over 20 bases. But he also had a huge power spike, hitting 26 out, driving in 88 runs, and scoring 100 more. He made his lone All-Star appearance that season and even got a few MVP votes. He also struck out 129 times in the process. "Sometimes, you start having success in one aspect and you kind of forget about the other things," Bradley explained. "When I hit home runs, I don't know if my responsibilities changed, but expectations changed a little bit. Therefore, I probably forgot a little bit about the other stuff. Part of the success of hitting home runs is that strike-outs come. That's not any excuse. That's just part of it.

"Part of striking out is when you strike out. It's one thing, maybe, to strike out when there's nobody on base. It's another thing to strike out with runners in scoring position. Timing is everything. If you can put the ball in play when there are runners in scoring position and maybe strikeout when there are two outs and nobody's on, that's two different things. Striking out is part of the game. To me it's more how you strike out. Are you striking out because you're swinging at bad pitches or are you striking out simply because guys are making good pitches on you? That's two different things."

Bradley admits that it was a combination of the two things for him throughout his career as he would end up having five 100-plus strikeout seasons. On that night in Boston, everything that Clemens threw up there worked. After striking out the side to open things up, he sent two more packing in the second.

He only got one K in the third before Spike Owen, a teammate of Clemens's at the University of Texas who would end up being reunited with him in Boston later in the season, led off the fourth inning with a single. In retaliation Clemens proceeded to strike out the next eight batters he faced. It was Owen, who never struck out more than 63 times in a season, who broke the string with a fly out to end the sixth inning. Clemens got some "help" in that fourth inning. After Bradley and Ken Phelps were handed a seat, Boston first baseman Don Baylor dropped a pop foul off the bat of Gorman Thomas. Given a second chance, Thomas promptly struck out, taking a called strike three. The eight consecutive strikeouts tied an American League record. Ryan did it twice with the Angels in 1973 and 1974 (Ron Davis also did it in 1981). Seaver had the major-league record, fanning ten straight San Diego Padres in April 1970 while pitching for the Mets.

With the seventh inning came perhaps a perfect argument for strikeouts being too harshly judged, that teams can have some success even while swinging and missing a lot. While Clemens was zipping along with all those Ks—he had 14 as the seventh began—the Mariners's Mike Moore was equally effective. He only had 3 strikeouts through six innings, but the biggest number was the zero he was putting up in the runs column. So when Thomas strode to the plate with two outs—2 K's, of course, to bring the game total to 16—in the top of the seventh, there was no score in the game. Clemens may have been nearly impossible to hit that night, but the veteran outfielder got hold of one and put it into the near-empty seats to give Seattle an improbable 1–0 lead.

"Our pitcher must've been doing something and we must've been playing OK defense," Bradley chuckled. "It wasn't like we were taking our offense out on the field. We were still competing as a team to try and win the game."

What would be the legacy of a game in which the starting pitcher struck out a record twenty batters but lost the game? The Mariners certainly weren't thinking about the strikeout mark in the dugout. This wasn't a no-hitter that had the collective offense wanting to make sure they weren't kept off the base paths entirely. Seattle was ahead with nine outs to go and its starter had his own shutout going, so the focus had nothing to do with avoiding the infamy of going down twenty times in one nine-inning contest. "The focus was still winning the game. It wasn't about statistics," Bradley insisted. "We were up 1–0. We were trying to win a ballgame. We were still in the game. If we win that game, 1–0, and Clemens strikes out twenty guys, are we still talking about that?"

Perhaps, but most likely in a much different context. It would probably be more a statistical curiosity than an amazing feat, more one of those oddities the game of baseball throws out from time to time, rather than one of the greatest pitching performances of all time. These historical considerations were rendered moot by the end of the seventh inning. Moore got two quick outs, inducing a pop-up from catcher Rich Gedman and a groundout off the bat of second baseman Marty Barrett. But then the bottom of the order started doing some damage. Center fielder Steve Lyons, hitting eighth, singled and moved to second when Glenn Hoffman, the shortstop, hitting ninth, walked. Then right fielder Dwight Evans, the leadoff hitter that night, smashed a three-run home run to put the game in the correct historical context.

"I was trying to battle a guy [Mike Moore] that's throwing a good game against us," Clemens said after the game. "The strikeouts just kept on coming. I knew something was happening because of the way the fans were reacting."

"He was using mainly fastballs. There was not much difference in his fastball from other games, just the location," Red Sox catcher Rich Gedman explained that night. "Guys were stretching for the ball, reaching for it. But as far as I'm concerned, those were unhittable."

Clemens whiffed two more in the eighth inning and then had to face the pesky Owens to lead off the ninth. When Owens went down swinging, Clemens was in the record books as part of a four-way tie, needing just one more strikeout in the next two batters to stand alone, ahead of the Hall of Famers he idolized. Bradley ended any added tension by looking at a called third strike for the second out of the ninth, Bradley's fourth K that night and Clemens's twentieth strikeout of the game.

"I still tell people I thought the pitch was inside, but twenty-one years later, it doesn't really matter," Bradley said. "That's the great thing about baseball. You get to do it a lot. Day in and day out. Some days you're going to be the Roger Clemens and some days you're going to be the Phil Bradley. You just hope you come out on the upper end more than you come out on the lower end. That's all."

Clemens came out on the upper end much more often than not in 1986. The Mariner game was the Rocket's fourth win in as many starts and he wouldn't pick up his first loss until the beginning of July, going 14–0 in his first fifteen starts. The performance against the Mariners was the second of four straight double-digit strikeout victories. He finished the year 24–4 with a 2.48 ERA, striking out 238, and walking just 77. But the Red Sox didn't, and couldn't, ride Clemens alone to the postseason that year. Bruce Hurst, the lefty who was nearly as tough against the Mariners the game following Clemens's record-breaker, finished fourth in the American League with his 2.99 ERA. Oil Can Boyd won sixteen games that year, and Al Nipper, while not as effective, also hit double-digits in victories. And in an interesting twist, Tom Seaver joined the staff via trade in his final months as a big leaguer.

"You had a little bit of everything," Bradley explained. "Bruce Hurst, back in the mid-80s, was a very accomplished left-handed pitcher. It wasn't like it was Roger Clemens and the other three. And Oil Can Boyd had his successes, too. The Red Sox had good starting pitching back then.

"I'll be honest with you. Reflecting back at that time, and with no disrespect to Al Nipper and Oil Can Boyd, but those were the two guys you had to try to do your damage off of. If you got hits off of Clemens and Bruce Hurst, that was just like an extra bonus. That's how it always is. If you have four or five starting pitchers, they're not all going to be the same. As a hitter, you have to try to take advantage of either the guys in the bottom part of the rotation or a guy who's having an off day."

Bradley did do that over the rest of the decade. The outfielder hit .471 against Boyd in his career and .351 against Nipper. He managed a decent 5 for 17 (.294) against Hurst. Against Clemens, that was a different story. Bradley went just 4 for 26 (.154) against the Rocket, with thirteen of those outs coming by way of the strikeout. He got his first hit off of the Red Sox ace later in that 1986 season, not long after the All-Star break. Clemens still won the game, improving to 16–2 on the year, but Bradley had his first knock in eleven tries. In July of 1987, Bradley had the kind of game you tell your grandchildren about, going 3 for 4 with a double and triple against Clemens. "I remember [manager] Dick Williams asked the night before if I wanted the day off and I said no," said Bradley, who had struck out three times in an earlier meeting that season against Clemens.

Bradley wouldn't really touch Clemens again. The Rocket had a complete-game 14-strikeout performance against Bradley and Seattle later in 1987, and Bradley would face him just one more time, with the Baltimore Orioles, in 1989. That resulted in one last collar for Bradley. "I'm telling you, the guy could throw any pitch for a strike," Bradley said. "What made him hard to hit in my estimation, he kind of threw, if it makes any sense, kind of at an angle. His ball cut across the strike zone on a diagonal, as opposed to coming straight at you. It's almost like he got off to the side of the ball a little bit.

"He was a special pitcher. Back then, another special pitcher was Bret Saberhagen. They were guys who threw hard, but threw with control so you weren't going to sit up there and say, 'If I stand up here long enough, they're going to walk me.' No, they aren't. You stay up there and you don't swing the bat, you're going to be in the hole 0–2 and trying to hit everything... The great pitchers of the game, if they're on their game, they are going to win most games. It's not because you as the hitter [were] not good. It's just that good pitching is going to beat good hitting. As good as these guys were, when they were on, they were on."

As on as Clemens was when Bradley dug in against him, he obviously had no idea just how good the right-hander would be. The 1986 season was Clemens's first Cy Young Award–winning effort, a breakthrough at age twenty-three. No one, least of all a player who is focused on competing daily over the course of a grueling baseball season, could predict what was to come. "When you play, you don't think about that," Bradley said. "You knew the guy was going to be a successful major-league player. To say, twenty-two years ago, he was going to still be around doing his thing, you didn't know."

Bradley knows now how Clemens compares with other great pitchers he faced, though there is one complication in trying to make those kinds of evaluations. Clemens was just getting started when Bradley hit against him. Guys like Seaver, Carlton, Jerry

Koosman, even Ryan, were on the way out, or at least on the down side of the career slope. "You could still tell that they were very good major-league pitchers, even at that age," Bradley said of the veteran starters he faced. "They didn't have the stuff they had had in their prime, but they could still get out the average major-league hitter. At the time that Clemens pitched, he was the best. But I faced him in his prime."

Bradley was out of the big leagues for good following the 1990 season, so he never got to see the reinvented veteran Clemens from the batter's box. But he's seen enough to realize that while there might be some similarities to what pitchers like Seaver did at the tail end, Clemens holds one advantage. "I think he's been able to maintain his velocity a little bit more than those other guys," Bradley said. "That might be the one difference. He's been able to maintain enough velocity that guys can't just sit in there and hit his off-speed pitch. They have to still respect his fastball."

The fastball. For better or for worse, that's what Roger Clemens is known for. The big Texas right-hander who can blow it by hitters at will, just like his idol and Lone Star State predecessor Nolan Ryan. With all due respect to the Express, Bradley's not sure that's a fair assessment. Linking those two up may not give Clemens's command the respect it deserves.

"I hit off Nolan Ryan further on in his career and I don't think [that works]," Bradley said. "If you're going to make a comparison, I would say Clemens was more like Tom Seaver than Nolan Ryan. People want to associate the strikeouts. When a guy strikes out twenty guys and walks none, he's more than just a power thrower. He's a power pitcher."

To Bradley that's what makes the game on April 29, 1986, so incredible, more remarkable than a no-hitter or any other single-game pitching feat. When Bradley was with the Phillies in 1988, Ryan took a no-no into the ninth. Bradley was also on the receiving end of Pascual Perez's five-inning, rain-shortened no-hitter that same season. They don't even belong in the same conversation as Clemens's record-breaker. "A no-hitter is phenomenal in its own right," Bradley said. "But what Clemens did that night, struck out twenty guys and didn't walk anybody, throwing as hard as anyone ever threw to me in the major leagues that night, to me, there's no comparison."

Bradley is still very much involved in the game of baseball. He is the special assistant to Don Fehr, the head of the Players Association. His main responsibility is to be Fehr's eyes and ears at the ballparks each summer. So Bradley spends a lot of time on the road, visiting and talking with players, building relationships. He might tell them there is no shame in failing in the game of baseball, that sometimes just being there for the great accomplishments—even if they are being accomplished at your expense—is more than enough.

"You know the picture in Sports Illustrated, with me standing there (taking the third strike for the record-breaking strikeout)? I've got that in my office," Bradley said. "Let me make it clear here. I'm glad I played in that game. I am not ashamed I struck out four times. I am proud to say I was part of that game. Whenever someone does something, a feat, and you're on the other side of the feat, that doesn't mean that you aren't a good player. It just means you weren't the better of the players that night. If that's the only thing I'm remembered for in the seven years I played, then so be it. And I'm not ashamed of it. It was a phenomenal night. It just so happened that I was the guy who struck out for the twentieth time."

TORII **HUNTER**

TORII HUNTER KNEW HE HAD been given a gift once he
heard the news. It came by way of an announcement
from the owner's box at Yankee Stadium on Sunday,
May 6, 2007.

Roger Clemens made it official, speaking to the
Yankee faithful in the Bronx that afternoon via the
video scoreboard. "Well, they came and got me out
of Texas and I can tell you it's a privilege to be back,"
Clemens said. "I'll be talking to y'all soon."

There was no surprise that Roger Clemens decided to make another late return to baseball for the
2007 season. And it would be difficult to find someone shocked that he chose to return to New York
over the Red Sox or Astros. Hunter may have been
more interested than most, especially once he perused
the Twins schedule and saw that Minnesota would be
heading to Yankee Stadium for four games in the beginning of July.

That would give him another chance—perhaps his
last one—to accomplish something that had eluded
him throughout his very successful career. He's logged
over 1,200 games of big-league time, surpassing the
1,200-hit plateau. He's slugged over 190 home runs

and stolen over 125 bases. He's been to the postseason with the Minnesota Twins four times, went to two All-Star Games and has a shelf full of Gold Gloves for his play in center field (six entering the 2007 season, to be exact). But there has been one achievement that has eluded the veteran star, the thing he hoped he'd finally be able to pick up in that visit to the Bronx in July 2007. Without including one playoff meeting, Hunter entered the 2007 season with an albatross-around-his-neck 0 for 22 against the Rocket. Then opportunity knocked one more time with Clemens's decision to return to the American League after three seasons over in the National League.

Clemens had rushed back to help rescue the Yankees in 2007. A series of injuries had decimated the pitching staff and New York was under .500 with the Red Sox threatening to run away with the AL East. So the Rocket accelerated his timetable, made a trio of minor-league starts, got delayed slightly by a balky groin, and made his season debut against the Pittsburgh Pirates on Saturday, June 9, just a month after announcing to the Yankee Stadium faithful he was coming back.

Clemens got the win against the Pirates, but it was an uneven performance, as he allowed 3 runs in six innings. He was up-and-down for the rest of the month, finishing June with a 5.32 ERA. There were more than a few whispers saying the Yankees had made a costly mistake in bringing back the forty-four-year-old. But Clemens would show he had more than a little left in the tank when the calendar turned to July.

It did seem like a perfect opportunity for Hunter. Clemens still looked very rusty and the Twins center fielder was having his best season since being an All-Star back in 2002. Hunter hit .302 up until the game against the Yankees and Clemens, with 17 homers, 63 RBIs, and 11 steals. He was optimistic, yet philosophical, about the opportunity to face his nemesis one more time. "For me, I get a chance to get that hit I need. I'm excited," said Hunter, who signed a big free-agent deal with the Los Angeles Angels following the 2007 season. "Me as an athlete, you don't want to be the guy who has no hits off anybody. I'm a better hitter, better player. I think I have a good chance getting that hit off him.

"I'm not that young kid any more. I'm older. I have more experience, I'm more under control. I understand the game. You get a hit three out of ten times, you're a hero. It's a game of failure. I'm going to try my best to get my hit, but I won't let it get me down. He's the only one who gets my number. He's struck out lots of people. If it's going to be one guy, I'll tell my grandkids Roger Clemens got me. It's something you have to cope with. If it doesn't happen, it was a good run, a good race. He's a Hall of Famer. Hang with 'em."

It didn't happen. Clemens, it seemed, chose July 2 to look like the pitcher the Yankees signed to help them climb back into the race. The right-hander went eight innings and allowed just 1 run on 2 hits. Once a strikeout machine who put up fairly big pitch counts, this Clemens was extremely efficient. He only threw ninety-seven pitches in the game, sixty-seven for strikes, while striking out four. It was win number

350 in Clemens's storied career and he hit that strati-
fied air with the second-lowest loss total in the history
of the game (only Cy Young had fewer losses when he
reached the 350-win plateau). Once again, Roger
Clemens was redefining the kind of pitcher he was
based on what he could still bring to the table.
Hunter knew ahead of time this wasn't going to be
the guy who dominated him—and everyone—in the
American League early on and probably not even the
pitcher who found success in the National League
over the previous three seasons.

"I think he's a different pitcher now," Hunter said
before facing him. "He probably has a different way
of getting it done. He's probably smarter. If I jumped
at the first pitch all the time, he might go slider off
the bat. I may have to watch how he goes at other
guys like me. I'll get my game plan from that. That's
how you feel them out. You watch and see what
they're doing. Once he gets on the mound, I'm going
to watch to see what he's doing. And trust me, I'll
have the scouting reports from everywhere."

They didn't prove to be much help. Hunter went
0 for 3 with a strikeout against this new version of
Clemens. That brought the total to 0 for 25 with 14
strikeouts. It's looking like Hunter will have to hang
with 'em. Of course it's not the first time Hunter faced
adversity in his career, particularly against Clemens.
Considering where he came from and the career he's
had, twenty-five at bats certainly won't keep the
ebullient center fielder down.

When the Minnesota Twins took Torii Hunter
with the twentieth overall pick in the 1993 draft out

of high school in Pine Bluff, Arkansas, they knew they were getting a very talented, if raw, athlete. Hunter was the type who excelled in every sport growing up and used to dream of a future in the NFL, not in Major League Baseball. Realistically, he hoped football would get him to college on a scholarship. Then the scouts were flocking to watch him play baseball and talk about him being a high draft pick began in earnest.

"Football was the sport I wanted to play," Hunter said. "But baseball, you get drafted in the first round, you kind of put that [football] on the back burner. I couldn't turn down the first round [bonus]. I started hearing that about baseball and I started thinking, 'Wait a minute, I might be playing the wrong sport.' I really had to shift a little bit and change directions. Actually, it worked out for the better."

That summer, Roger Clemens was already pitching in his tenth major-league season. Hunter was playing in the Gulf Coast League. Digging in against Roger Clemens wasn't exactly something in the front of his mind. In Pine Bluff the only station that showed baseball while Hunter was growing up was WGN, the Cubs superstation. So it should come as no surprise that the one baseball player Hunter did look up to—while his other idols were all football players—was Andre Dawson. Roger Clemens was someone Hunter obviously had heard of, but he'd mostly only get glimpses of him in All-Star Games or the playoffs, since Clemens didn't face a National League opponent in the regular season until the advent of interleague play in 1997.

"When I was younger, I didn't dream of facing Roger Clemens, but I knew of him," Hunter explained. "I remember Andre Dawson and that's what really got me started playing baseball. Roger Clemens was a name you always heard about as one of the dominant pitchers in the game. The Rocket. That's all I remember. The Rocket. When I got drafted in 1993 out of high school, you always heard about him. Then, before you know it, you're facing this guy."

Before you know it was really six years. It wasn't that easy of a trip for Hunter. Four summers into his pro career, it was unclear what kind of big leaguer, if any, Hunter would be. He spent parts of three seasons in Double-A New Britain. After having a nice first full season back in 1994, hitting .293 in the Midwest League, he had trouble keeping his average up. He hit just .246 in the Florida State League in 1995 and .263 in his first taste of Double-A in '96.

At one point, in 1997 just prior to his first call-up, Hunter even considered calling it quits. He hit just .231 that season with a .641 OPS and began to question just how much he wanted a future in baseball. And as much as being competitive was motivation for him, the long grind of a baseball season meant that he had to find a more personal attachment to the game itself.

"When you play baseball every day, like you do in pro ball, I had to dig deep to find the true love I had for baseball," Hunter said. "I kept plugging away because it was a sport and I was being competitive. And I worked hard. I worked very hard. I didn't really find the love for baseball until 1997."

To be precise, it was August 22, 1997. Remember in the movie Bull Durham, Crash Davis wows everyone on the A-level Durham Bulls bus about how he spent eighteen days in the big leagues once? He describes it as a Shangri-la, of sorts. He's more or less on the money, at least from the eyes of a minor leaguer trying to get there. Hunter spent a whopping four days in the big leagues in 1997. But it was enough to ignite a passion in the outfielder, a realization that all the ups-and-downs, all the long road trips and nondescript minor-league towns would be worth it if he could get back to the top level full-time. It was a cup of coffee with a permanent caffeine jolt.

"The Twins had a plan," Hunter said. "They saw I was down. I actually wanted to give up in 1997 because it seemed like it wasn't working out. I wasn't moving fast enough. The game was kind of slow to me. It took me awhile, but when I got called up to the big leagues, I think that really changed my mind-set. When I got called up, it was amazing. I saw everything I was working for. Hanging out with Kirby Puckett, hanging out with Otis Nixon and all these guys who were on the team at the time.

"I got called up to Baltimore. Just being around the game, going out there at Camden Yards, pinch-running for Matt Lawton in 1997, seeing 55,000 people screaming and yelling in a big stadium under the lights. I said, 'Man, this is a new-found love for real.'

"When I got sent back down, you saw something totally different in me. My numbers were up; my home run totals were up. I played the game differently. It wasn't that I wasn't working hard or playing hard [before], but I was actually [becoming] a student of the game. I was really trying to get to that goal, which was the major leagues."

Hunter began the 1998 season back in Double-A, but got called back up to Minnesota at the end of April. Camden Yards was the site of his first big-league game, and he got another first—his first major-league hit—in Baltimore on May 1. He picked up his first RBIs as well during his six-game stay in the big leagues. When he was sent down to Double-A, he kept raking and earned an eventual promotion to Triple-A, where he hit .337 over twenty-six games to go along with a .543 slugging percentage, his career high to that point. For the season Hunter matched his career best in homers with 10 and added 31 doubles, beginning to show that he was ready to realize the potential the Twins saw when they took him with the twentieth pick in the draft.

Hunter began to settle into the Twins outfield, or so it seemed, in 1999. During that season Hunter amassed 384 at bats over the course of the season, hitting .255 with 9 homers and 10 steals. He also picked up his first three at bats against Clemens, going 0 for 3 with a strikeout against the Yankees at the Metrodome in August.

It was actually the second time in a week the Twins had faced the Rocket, getting blanked, 2–0, on August 14, in New York. Clemens pitched 8⅔ innings of shutout ball. Hunter sat and watched. The Twins manager of the time, Tom Kelly, was a big-time situational lineup guy. That meant with one of the best right-handed pitchers of all time on the mound, the

Twins lineup featured a slew of left-handed hitters. "They didn't let me play because they didn't think I was ready to face him," said Hunter, recalling one of the many things he and Kelly did not see eye-to-eye on. Tom Kelly didn't believe a right-hander should face a tough right-hander like Roger Clemens. "Us being so young, he didn't let too many young guys play who were right-handers. So I didn't get to face him the first time."

Looking back, Hunter is of two minds about that day off. One the one hand, he's the ultimate competitor, and at age twenty-two, he was full of the bravado that made him want to grab a bat and take his hacks. On the other, especially after watching Clemens carve up the lefty-heavy lineup that day, there was a part of Hunter that was relieved to sit that one out.

"When you're watching him and the way he carved our team up—he sliced us up—just sitting there watching, you think, 'Man, maybe I should have the day off. Maybe I'm glad he took me out,'" Hunter said. "You're saying that to yourself, but the competitiveness in you, you want to go out there because that may be the day you get a hit off of Roger Clemens. You never know. Somewhere in the back of your head, there's a little devil saying, 'You can't hit him' and 'You better be glad you had the day off.' That little voice is telling me that and I was kind of glad that day that I took the day off."

He didn't have that luxury seven days later. The Twins and Yankees played more often those days, before unbalanced schedules provided many more meetings between teams in the same division. Back in the Metrodome on August 21, Kelly let his young center fielder take a crack at the legend. It turned out to be the first of many times Hunter went hitless off of Clemens, but Hunter admits that the first time, Clemens's presence got him out as much, if not more, than his stuff.

"Mentally, I told myself, 'That's Roger Clemens!' As a twenty-two-year-old kid, a young guy just coming up, you get the chance to face a Hall of Famer, already. If he had quit at that time, he's a Hall of Famer," Hunter recalled. "I actually got a chance to face him and I was nervous before the game. I'm like, 'Man, Roger Clemens.' We had to go out and face Roger Clemens. Somewhere around that time, he developed the split-finger. That made him even more nasty. I'm over here, having to face Roger Clemens. I'm kind of nervous. I'm like, 'I have to face him. Here we go.' It was more like an intimidation factor that got me."

In addition to the Clemens aura, the right-hander undoubtedly had a good scouting report on Hunter. The young Twins that year had a strict game plan they had to adhere to. The marching orders were to go the other way whenever humanly possible. To Hunter it meant doing it more than he felt was possible, but he was a young, unestablished player trying to show his skipper he belonged. For a veteran like Clemens, it made Hunter easy pickings. "Every pitcher in the American League knew what I was trying to do," Hunter said. "Every pitcher knew what we had to do. Roger brought that extra aura with him. I was trying to fight it and go the other way and show Tom Kelly I could hit. That was part of it."

In the early stages of his career, Hunter did have the benefit of some veteran tutelage on the Twins. Even if he was frustrated by the Tom Kelly philosophy, having accomplished hitters like Paul Molitor, Terry Steinbach and Kirby Puckett around to shepherd him through challenges like facing Clemens was a huge plus. In their combined careers Molitor, Steinbach, and Puckett had 243 at bats against Roger Clemens. They also had a fair share of success, especially when compared with other hitters from their era.

Molitor, who gained entrance into the Hall of Fame in 2004 thanks to his 3,319 hits and career .306 average, hit .308 against Clemens, making him one of the few players with a higher average against the Rocket than his career mark. Puckett hit .296 in eighty-one at bats against Clemens and was a 2001 inductee into Cooperstown. He retired before Hunter came up, but he never strayed too far from the Twins family. Steinbach wasn't as successful, hitting .255 in fifty-five at bats. But the catcher did homer twice against Clemens and finished his fourteen-year career with 1,453 hits. When guys like that talked hitting, you listened, especially when you're a young hitter trying to establish yourself the way Hunter was.

"When I had Molitor and Steinbach, they helped in figuring ways to get [Clemens]," said Hunter, who also had help from Molitor when he was the Twins bench coach in 2000 and 2001. "They'd tell me: Jump on him early, you don't want to see that splitty. I'd try and I'd foul him off. I was young, trying to go the other way. I'd foul pitches off, now I'm 0–2 here. Molly always said, jump on him early and don't miss.

That's why I talked to him. I would talk to Kirby, he'd say the same thing. Get on him early and don't miss it. Guys like that make one mistake. Don't miss the pitch because he's not going to give you another chance."

The following year, Hunter had three more chances against Clemens on three occasions, though it was a different Hunter who dug in against the Rocket in the last matchup of the season. Hunter struggled in 2000, including two performances against Clemens. In the first one, on April 24, he struck out twice and grounded out in a Twins 7–3 win at Yankee Stadium. In late July, the Yankees came to the Metrodome. Clemens tossed seven shutout innings, with Hunter striking out in the second, walking and stealing a base in the fourth, and grounding out to short in the sixth. The Twins would go on to win that game, 7–3.

Though Hunter was more or less a part of the Twins everyday lineup, playing in ninety-nine games and collecting 336 at bats, he struggled for most of the year, even against pitchers not named Clemens. So the Twins sent him down at the end of July to let him get his feet back under him. It worked. Hunter would hit .343 with 5 homers, 8 doubles, 3 triples, and 31 RBIs the rest of the way after being called back up. He never returned to the minor leagues again. "I had regained my confidence and started hitting," Hunter said. "I was hitting well. When I came back up, I was confident."

He was no longer the young outfielder intimidated by the likes of Roger Clemens. His newfound attitude was put to the test on September 3, 2000, when his Twins faced Clemens's Yankees for the final time that season. Clemens, again, was in top form, going eight innings on the rainy Sunday afternoon, allowing just an earned run and striking out 8. Hunter, for his part, took another "0 for," going hitless in three plate appearances. But this time he wasn't nearly as helpless as he may have seemed earlier in the year. Hunter flew out to center field in the third, the first time he managed to get the ball out of the infield against Clemens.

Then came the pivotal at bat in the fifth inning. If not for the official scorer at Yankee Stadium that day, Hunter wouldn't be carrying a .000 against Roger Clemens (and perhaps this chapter would not have been written). Hunter hit a ball past third baseman Scott Brosius that was ruled a two-base error. Perhaps the official scorer had seen Brosius make too many outstanding defensive plays; he had won a Gold Glove at the hot corner the previous year in 1999, after all. Whatever the reason, it went down as an "E5" and the hitless streak continued. To his credit Hunter walked in the tenth inning, stole second, and scored the winning run on a Denny Hocking single. The pitcher? Mariano Rivera, who will undoubtedly join Clemens in Cooperstown one day.

"I hit him well that day. I just didn't get a hit," said Hunter, who would also strike out in the seventh against Clemens. "I hit one past Scott Brosius they called an error, which I thought was a double. It was a two-base error. I'll never forget that. I hit it down the line. He dove for it and they called it an error and it was 100 percent a hit."

Not that Hunter realized that would be the closest thing to a base hit he'd have against the Rocket at the time. For the record he was officially 0 for 11 with 5 strikeouts. But as much as Hunter struggled, especially in 2000, the Twins fared well against Clemens. Their center fielder may have taken the collar for the three games, but they went 3–0 in those games, twice beating the reliever who followed Clemens into the game. Not too shabby for a team that went 69–93 while the Yankees were going on to their fourth World Series title in five years. "I really never paid attention [to my numbers against him] because we beat him a couple of times that year. I remember that," Hunter said.

Hunter would face Clemens just one time in 2001, the season the Yankees would go on to lose the World Series to the Arizona Diamondbacks and in many ways end their dynasty. The Twins faced Clemens on May 9 and he was once again masterful. The Rocket struck out 8, walked just 1, and yielded just 4 hits in eight shutout innings. Hunter added 2 more strikeouts to his career record, going down in the third and seventh while sandwiching in a fielder's choice in between. And this time, Clemens got the victory. Hunter looks at this philosophically, realizing that a guy with over 4,600 career strikeouts is going to ring up even the better hitters in the game from time-to-time. "Everybody is going to strike out against Roger Clemens," Hunter said. "Even the worst pitcher is going to get you. I'd rather strike out against Roger Clemens than the worst pitcher."

He would have more opportunities, though if there was going to be a year for Hunter, who was 0 for 14 at that point, to break the schneid against Clemens, it was 2002. It was a coming-out season for the Twins center fielder. He finished the season with 29 home runs and 23 steals. He won his second Gold Glove (he had a streak of six in a row going heading into the 2007 season), finished sixth in the American League Most Valuable Player voting, and made his first All-Star appearance. Most people probably recall one of the most famous All-Star Game catches, courtesy of Hunter, who leapt in front of the center field wall to rob none other than Barry Bonds of a Midsummer Classic home run. Hunter had been a decent player leading up to this season, but he put it all together in 2002. The reason? It was simple, according to Hunter. He just went out and played ball.

"I was just going out there, not thinking about much," Hunter said. "In the past I was always thinking about my swing. I tried to do everything everyone wanted me to do. During the game I'd try to get my foot down, try to hit the ball to right field when the ball is inside. I tried to do all of that in my previous years. But that year, in 2002, I told myself in the offseason before that when the season started, I wasn't going to listen to anybody. I was going to use my God-given ability. I was going to just see ball, hit ball, and swing the bat. Hard. I actually did that in 2002. I went out there and didn't think, just see ball, hit ball. I didn't have good mechanics—I may have had good mechanics, you never know—I just didn't look at my tape. I just used my God-given ability and it actually worked in 2002. You can overthink a lot. Overthinking in baseball can get you hurt. That's what I had done in previous years. That year, I didn't think about anything and I just played the game."

Unfortunately, it didn't work against Clemens in the one time the two crossed paths. The Twins ran into a buzz saw of a Clemens on May 19 in Yankee Stadium. The right-hander went eight shutout innings, gave up 4 hits and 2 walks, and struck out 13, one of the well over a hundred times Clemens has fanned ten or more in his illustrious career. Hunter was his victim three times, though he did manage to fly out to center for one of his four at bats. "He struck out 13? I had no chance, then," Hunter laughed. "Sometimes, as a hitter, we'll all tell you, sometimes you just have to take it on the chin. You tip your cap to the pitcher.

"I remember them putting my picture up there three times for striking out. The fans, they hang your picture up like for the dead, like you've been carved up or killed. I remember looking up and wondering why my face was up there three times. That's one of the days, you just have to tip your cap and say, 'OK, Roger Clemens is one of the best pitchers in the game.' He struck out 13 and I was just 3 of them. You go out there and do your best, but the guy is a legend. He's either going to get you or you're going to get him, and he usually gets you more than you get him. Maybe the next day, I hit somebody pretty hard. That's when I started tipping my hat to guys."

(For the record Hunter's memory serves him well. After a day off the Twins returned home to Minnesota to play the Texas Rangers. Hunter went 2 for 5 with 5 RBIs.)

The 2003 season wasn't any better for the Hunter side of the Hunter-Clemens matchup. Their lone regular-season meeting came on April 18, early in that season. Clemens went six innings, struck out 8 and allowed 1 run. Hunter went 0 for 2 with a walk and 2 strikeouts to bring him to 0 for 20. Gone also were the days that Hunter's collar became easily forgettable because of a Twins win. The Yankees won 11–4, their third straight victory, dating back to 2001, against Minnesota, with Clemens on the hill.

Hunter would get a bonus chance. The Yankees, once again, won the AL East in 2003. The Twins won the AL Central, their second of three straight division titles. Hunter has been a solid contributor in the postseason for the Twins, with a .300 career average. He hit .429 against the Yankees in that series. None of that, however, came against Clemens.

It was Game 3 of the best-of-five series and the Yankees and Twins had split the first two games at Yankee Stadium. Minnesota had a chance, back at home in the Metrodome, where they had gone 48–32 during the regular season, to send New York home early for the second straight season. (The Yankees lost to the Angels in the ALDS the previous year. The Angels then beat the Twins in the ALCS and went on to win the World Series.) Unfortunately for the Twins, Clemens and the Yankees bullpen stood in the way.

Clemens's postseasons have not been as overwhelmingly dominant as the rest of his career. He's been mortal at times, though his overall numbers—12–8, 3.75 ERA, 173 strikeouts, in 199 innings—are nothing to sneeze at. In this ALDS game, though, he was good enough to start to put an end to the Twins title hopes.

Clemens went six strong innings, allowing just a single run. The bullpen took it from there and the Yankees went on to dispatch the Twins in four games. They eventually would reach the World Series for the sixth time in eight years, only to lose it to the upstart Florida Marlins. Who can forget the Marlins dugout giving Clemens a standing ovation when he left his Series start, thinking it would be his final one before retirement? Everyone knows what happened after that (creating possibilities for several more chapters in this book).

"We choked. We had them on the ropes," Hunter admitted. "We went back to our place and we choked. With everything on the line, all their ability came out. All cylinders clicked once they found they were on the ropes. We had a chance to beat the Evil Empire. We were making minimum wage and they were billionaires, and we couldn't get it done. We thought we had a nice story there. We thought we could beat this giant and the giant fell on top of us."

Clemens was the Goliath in Game 3, not that the Twins didn't have opportunities to fell him. Trailing 3–1 in the sixth inning, Hunter came to the plate with a runner on second base and two outs. Hunter had gone 0 for 2 against his nemesis, with a strikeout. He had a chance to erase all of it with one swing in that sixth inning, Clemens's last of the night. One swing from Hunter—not out of the realm of possibility as he had hit 26 regular-season home runs—would have tied the score and sent the Metrodome into a frenzy. But Hunter grounded out to end the inning.

"You can hit the ball hard, but you have to have a little luck, too," Hunter said about the playoff matchup, though the sentiment works for his entire career against Clemens. "Some balls are hit hard against him; I just didn't have any luck. That's just one guy I just had no luck with, that's Roger. You'd think I could get a little luck after I struck out so many times. I felt good the whole series, but then I just couldn't get it done. In baseball you can't do it [all] yourself."

Thinking back, Hunter can only shake his head and wonder about what made Clemens tick. For a guy allegedly on his way out, he sure didn't pitch like it. "Any great pitchers in the game, you have to create runs," Hunter said. "It's going to be hard to get to that next base with Roger Clemens or Pedro Martinez on the mound. You have to create a way to get to that extra base, either stealing or sacrificing. Every run off of Roger Clemens is very important. It's going to be hard to get that three-run homer or two-run double. We were trying to do that, but we couldn't get it done. He wouldn't allow it.

"This guy, at the time, was forty. He was supposed to go down. He didn't go down. He actually went up. He got better as he got older. Most pitchers go down, their velocity goes down. Roger was still pumping 94, 95, 96, maybe 97 sometimes. Nobody could figure out how he was throwing like that, but I heard he was a hard worker and he tries to stay in shape. He tries to keep up with these young guys. He is a freak of nature. I don't get it. I have all the heart in the world, but when Roger Clemens is up there, I'm like, 'Man, how come I can't hit him?' "

It seemed likely that Hunter would never get another chance to answer that question. The 2003 season,
of course, was not Clemens's last. But it was his final
one in Yankee pinstripes. The Rocket went home to
Texas and signed with the Houston Astros during the
off-season. Just to prove Hunter's point about not
slipping, Clemens went out and won another Cy
Young Award in 2004 and helped the Astros reach
the World Series in 2005.

None of this had an impact on Hunter at all. The
Astros and Twins didn't meet up in interleague play
in 2004 or 2005. The Twins, while perennial playoff
contenders, couldn't get over the hump and make it
to the World Series in order to get a postseason crack
at any National League opponent. Hunter was sure
he'd be wearing that "0 for" forever. "For three years
I'm thinking I'm never going to face this guy," Hunter
said. "He's going to retire."

But then came 2006 and a chance for redemp-
tion. Clemens signed late with the Astros and made
three minor-league starts on his way to returning to
the Houston rotation. His first big-league outing was
scheduled for June 22, an interleague affair against
none other than the Minnesota Twins. "I was pissed
off. I was pissed off he came back and then we had to
play Houston," Hunter deadpanned. "I was hoping
we didn't get to face him."

Perhaps Hunter was only half kidding, but he
claims he was eager to get one last—if it was the final
one—crack at breaking the Clemens code. With
triple-digit home runs and stolen bases, along with
more than 1,200 hits on his big-league resume,

Hunter no longer fears any pitcher and believes, down to his core, that in any given at bat, he's a match for any major-league hurler. "At this time now, I feel I can face anybody, so when I had the chance to get Roger Clemens, I said, 'Believe me, I'm going to try to get this hit right now,'" Hunter recounted.

He didn't even know how much futility he had endured against Clemens until the Twins got to Houston. Obviously, he knew he hadn't fared well against the future Hall of Famer, but it wasn't until a reporter approached him about it that he knew just how big an "0 for" he was carrying. "I came to the realization in Houston when one of the guys from ESPN, Pedro Gomez, told me I had no hits off of Roger Clemens and we were facing him in two days," Hunter said. "That's when I found out."

Presumably, it was a good time to put a one in the hit column. It was Clemens's first big-league start in eight months. He had thrown a total of just 14⅔ minor-league frames to get ready for this game. And while he'd defied the age gods for many years, he was forty-three at the time. Eventually, Father Time had to catch up, right? Even Clemens has said his body doesn't respond the way it once did. Hunter was in the perfect position, during a trip to Minute Maid Park in Houston, to be the beneficiary of a rusty Rocket.

"I've got to get a hit off of him. Now, here's my chance to face him in Houston. This year, I'm getting a hit off of him," Hunter told himself. "When you step in the box, it's just you and him. On the field you're not thinking about the outside stuff, though it gave me an edge. I'm really pumped up trying to get you. I have to show people I can hit you, I have to show myself I can hit you. It didn't work out."

Though the Twins won the game behind young lefty Francisco Liriano and Hunter did deliver an RBI single off of reliever Fernando Nieve in the seventh, Hunter could not get that base knock. He went 0 for 2, with a fly out to center field following Justin Morneau's one-out double in the second inning and a strikeout in the third after the Twins had scored a couple of runs and had runners at first and second. Clemens only went five in his debut, so there would be no third time around for Hunter.

"That [second] at bat, I had a great at bat, fouling balls off. I'm telling myself, 'I'm going to get him.' I felt good with all the swings," Hunter said. "Then he threw me a split-finger in the dirt. A lot of right-handed hitters can't hit a right-handed split-finger. That's one of the toughest pitches in the game. He threw the split-finger and I was like, 'Man, I can't believe this. He got me again.' I had told myself I wasn't going to let him get me this time. I wanted my first hit to be a home run and I was swinging so hard for the fence because I feel like I'm a better hitter, I'm more mature at the plate and I'm not intimidated by him. If he made a mistake, I knew I would get him. Believe me, he didn't make a mistake and this guy hadn't pitched in so long."

Hunter was unsure whether he would ever get another crack at Clemens, "just to get my dignity." That's how it was with Clemens in the latter stages of his career, with everyone waiting to find out if and when the Rocket would return. Hunter got his answer, but it simply added three more at bats to the career of coming up empty. Hunter, never one to hang his head over anything, certainly isn't losing any sleep, especially considering he's not exactly alone among hitters in not being able to master the master right-hander.

"I'm not ashamed or anything," Hunter said. "As baseball players, we know we always have tomorrow. So if I go 0 for 2 against Roger Clemens, in that same series, I may go 3 for 4 and I'm the one actually winning. For the whole series we play a three-game set, Roger might get me the first time, but I might go 10 for the next 12, so I'm winning, I'm helping my team win. It doesn't matter what Roger Clemens did, that's an individual goal. That's the way I looked at it. This guy got me in Houston, so the next couple of games, I'm going to get somebody else.

"If I can't get Roger, one of the best pitchers ever to play the game, OK. The other guys will have to get punished. If you ask most of the hitters out there, when you face Roger Clemens, you don't make your money off of that guy. You make your money off the next couple of guys."

While that team-first notion is most definitely sincere, there's also no doubt that the competitor in Hunter was burning to get that base hit. If there's one more round to this, if Hunter can get another last shot, would he do anything to get that big zero off his stat line? Almost, but he would draw the line at bunting for that first hit. "No, I have too much pride. I can't do that," Hunter said. "If I didn't have a hit and I laid one down, people would've been talking about me forever. I would talk about me. For my first hit I was trying to make it a home run. That would've taken everything away. I wouldn't have thought about the 14 strikeouts I'd had in the past. I would've thought about that home run off of Roger Clemens. Then I wouldn't want to face him anymore because I'd want to end on a good note. I'd say I got the flu or something."

Over all those years, with twenty-five (twenty-eight if you throw in the postseason) at bats, there is one other thing Hunter hasn't had with Clemens, other than a base hit. He's never had a conversation with the future Hall of Famer. The one time Hunter may have had the opportunity to at least chat with the right-hander a bit would've been an All-Star Game. But the lone year Hunter was chosen in 2002, Clemens was not part of the American League pitching staff. They've exchanged a nod, a one-liner, in passing, but Hunter was told from the outset of his big-league career that Clemens was not exactly the chatty type, particularly with "the enemy." He's relaxed a bit in the latter stages of his career, but it's doubtful anyone would identify Roger Clemens as a touchy-feely sensitive type.

"I've never had a conversation with Roger in my whole life," Hunter said. "I'll walk past Roger, I would say something like, 'Roger, you're nasty,' while he's doing an interview and he'll just smile or whatever. But I've never had a conversation with him.

"I didn't think he really spoke to hitters or opposing players. I didn't want him to get upset. I had heard stories that you really don't want to talk to

Roger and Roger won't talk to you. So I went by what people said and I didn't want to go out of the way and say something to him. If he said something to me that was out of hand, then we'd have a confrontation."

Now, before you think Hunter is just blowing smoke, remember where he comes from. Most would see someone as imposing as Roger Clemens and cower immediately. But Hunter faced larger threats back in the day in Pine Bluff and doesn't blink as he sets up the hypothetical throw down. He also is clear to point out the difference between fear and intimidation. Yes, he admits, he was greatly intimidated by Clemens early in his career. But Torii Hunter fears no man, though he's never been one to charge the mound.

"I don't fight on the field. I'd have to get him off the field," Hunter said with a wink. "I'm from the hood. I've fought way bigger guys than that in the hood, believe me. It's not the fact I'm scared of Roger physically. I'm not scared of him as a pitcher, but I think he is very intimidating as a pitcher, not as a person."

That being said, Hunter would jump at the chance to sit down with Clemens and talk about their two dozen or so matchups. Perhaps it would be something once the Rocket actually officially retires, so he wouldn't have any concern about revealing any secrets, about letting his guard down and taking away his edge. With both Hunter and Clemens spending time during the off-season at least in Texas (granted, Hunter's in Dallas and Clemens is in the Houston area), it's not difficult to envision a summit of sorts to discuss the big zero Clemens has thrown up against Hunter over the course of his career.

"I would love to sit down and talk to him and see what he saw in my swing," Hunter said. "He saw that I was trying to pull off and things like that, trying to swing hard to try to get him, so he went to the splitty. I thought maybe he went to the splitty because he saw me pulling off a lot. It was always the splitty. It wasn't the fastball. The fastball, I usually could foul off. When he threw the splitty, that was it. That was game time."

Hunter thinks it was game time especially for right-handed hitters. Lefties may tell you it's no picnic hitting Clemens, either, but Hunter felt it was an even bigger disadvantage when he tried to dig in against the Rocket. "With right-handed hitters against right-handed pitchers, it's hard enough. Their arm is right behind you, when they release, the ball is right at your body, your head," said Hunter, who has hit fifteen points lower against righties than against southpaws in his career. "And Clemens would throw up and in. You're thinking inside and you pull off a little, he throws the splitter or cutter, you'll miss it.

"For a lefty the ball is away from you and you can stay on it a little longer. You don't have to move away. The natural instinct for a right-handed hitter when the ball is behind me, when it seems like the ball is coming at you, your body opens up a little. That's how Roger did it. He developed that cutter later and could come with the cutter away. He'd throw a lot more cutters and splitters away later. He'd throw splitters all the time; I'd say, 'Man, his arm is going to fall off!' But it never did. I used to see Rocket blow everybody away. But when I got to the major leagues, I'd look for the fastballs, but it was all splitters. You knew you would get it, but it was tough. It looks like a fastball, down the middle, then right before you swing, it ducks, like the ball had eyes. Like a cartoon. It was pretty funny...No, it wasn't funny at all."

THE NEXT
GENERATION

JOHNNY DRENNEN

JOHNNY DRENNEN WAS FINISHING HIS senior season of high school and preparing for the First-Year Player Draft. He would hear his name called early, taken in the supplemental first round by the Cleveland Indians. Little did he know that on the same Tuesday one year later, in the southern city of Lexington, Kentucky, he'd face a living legend and future Hall of Fame pitcher. And it was beyond even his wildest dreams to think he'd take one of the best pitchers of all time deep.

To understand how Drennen, a high school outfielder from San Diego, and Roger Clemens crossed paths on June 6, 2006, you have to go back to the off-season between the 2005 and 2006 seasons. It was another Hot Stove season dominated by WILL HE OR WON'T HE? headlines regarding Clemens. Will he come back for another season? Will he come back with the Houston Astros? Will he come back for the entire season?

It was the third straight off-season that everyone got to play that waiting game. It started following the 2003 season, Clemens's last with the New York Yankees. His final start appeared to be in the World

Series, when the eventual champions, the Florida Marlins, gave Clemens a standing ovation when he left the mound. But Clemens changed his mind, deciding to join the Astros and his good friend Andy Pettitte, who also left the Yankees following the 2003 season to return home.

After 2004 Clemens was supposedly 99 percent retired, but he came back in 2005 to help Houston reach the World Series for the first time in the franchise's history. After the Astros were swept by the White Sox, Clemens once again said he "considered himself retired." Then, not to the surprise of anyone, he reconsidered. The Yankees, Red Sox, and Texas Rangers, along with the Astros, were trying to woo Clemens back for one more go-round.

He didn't agree to a 2006 contract until June 1, when he and the Astros agreed to a $22 million contract (to be fair, it was prorated from the date that he joined the team, so he collected a bit more than $12 million in 2006) to pitch for the rest of the season. Once he finally signed, the decision was that he would make his 2006 major-league debut on June 22. Prior to that, though, he would head on a magical mystery tour through the minor leagues, a Rocket trip through three rungs of the Astros system to get him ready to begin his twenty-third season in the big leagues.

"I have to now take the next step to get my body ready to come back, to be effective, win games, and do what I'm used to doing, and that's being extremely competitive at a high level," said Clemens, who had made two starts in March during the World Baseball Classic. "My body feels good. Condition-wise, I'm great. I need some game experience. I haven't felt soreness in my legs like actual game situations."

The first stop was in Lexington, home of the Legends, the Astros Low-A affiliate in the South Atlantic League. Most rosters in the Sally League are made up of kids, like Drennen, who were drafted just the previous June and are less than a year removed from their senior years of high school or junior years of colleges. Facing the Rocket is a fantasy, something they might be able to do on Xbox, but almost certainly not on the field, considering Clemens's age and how far these minor leaguers have to go to get to the big leagues. By the time a teenager in his first full season of pro ball got to the big leagues, logic seemed to say, Clemens would've long since ridden off into the sunset.

Opportunity presented itself when Clemens began his "rehab" in Lexington. He started in the Sally League for two reasons. One, it was a good way to ease back into competitive pitching, facing first-year pros who likely wouldn't present too much of a challenge for a pitcher of Clemens's quality in the early going. Two, Clemens's oldest son, Koby—a member of the same 2005 draft class as Drennen—was the third baseman for the Legends. Not only could Clemens start getting into game shape, he could spend some quality time with his son.

The plan was for Clemens to go three innings in his 2006 debut against the Lake County Captains, the Indians affiliate in the South Atlantic League. Applebee's Park, the Legends's home, is a nice size (6,000 capacity) for a Sally League stadium. But it certainly had to brace for the onslaught of fans—9,222 in total when all was said and done—and members of the media—more than 130 credentials were issued for the game—who swarmed into Kentucky for the start. All eyes, thanks to the decision by ESPN to nationally televise the Rocket's outing, turned to Lexington to watch Clemens's debut.

Drennen batted third in the Captains lineup that day. In many ways he may have been the perfect person to take advantage of being placed in the right place at the right time. Spend any time with Drennen and you definitely sense a little bit of a "surfer" vibe. That's not at all surprising considering he spent almost all of his childhood in San Diego. The beach was a second home of sorts for Drennen, an escape from reality. "Going to the beach is a time to let the mind be free and just relax," he said. "It's nothing I take seriously. It's just something I do for fun. I'm here, so why not just go and enjoy it. When there's time, there's time.

"I used to do the body board thing. Still do. I never surfed because you could get injured. Body boarding is safer, in my eyes. A lot of guys do it, but you have to know your limits. I don't mess with anything big anymore. It's not this macho thing anymore like when you were in high school. Now, there are risks involved. Well, there were risks then, but now you realize what they are."

There is the attitude that comes along with the beach scene, of course. Drennen, with his tousled blonde hair and "no worries" outlook on life, fits in perfectly. "I'm just a real easygoing guy," he said. "I just seem to deflect things, let things happen. Everyone gets old. There are going to be challenges in life, so you can't really get too bent out of shape about things or let people bend you out of shape. It's just staying level-minded. At times I have challenges with it. It's always a work in progress."

If the beach was his second home, Drennen quickly realized his first home was the baseball field. Playing competitive baseball in Southern California is about as easy as finding a beach, with the game going on year-round. Drennen quickly found himself playing as much as he could, as often as he could. He played other sports, but they all were left behind by the time he reached high school. "It's not that I realized I was any good. I realized I loved to play the game," he said. "I don't consider the beach a passion. I consider the game of baseball a passion."

Drennen was plenty good. But talent alone doesn't get you noticed and drafted in the first round out of high school. Raw skills and a laid-back attitude won't get you ready to make the transition to professional baseball and they certainly won't have you prepared to face perhaps the greatest right-handed pitcher in baseball history.

"My initial reaction when I met with him in his house with his family was that it might be a concern [his surfer attitude]," said Jason Smith, the Indians scout who signed Drennen. "I try to dig into the makeup. I think it's very, very important, maybe the most important asset a prospect can have. Sometimes I dig too deep into that. My first reaction was that it might be a concern because he was a little bit aloof and had a little bit of a surfer mentality."

Smith would eventually learn that Drennen wasn't just a beach bum. That's what sets Drennen apart. He may be the first superdisciplined surfer dude in the game. He comes by the work ethic and commitment honestly. His father, John Sr., is a former Navy SEAL, an explosive ordinance diver, who served in the first Iraq war. Drennen was fairly fortunate. Many military families are constantly on the move, but John Jr. was born in Hawaii, moved to Florida at around age three, then on to San Diego at age five. Almost all of his memories are of his time in Southern California, and he recalls the lessons taught by his father about hard work and responsibility.

"As a kid, you go through it. It's being disciplined and being held accountable for actions, knowing when you're doing wrong," he said. "He was always one to confront me on it and discipline me to where I'd grow up to be a successful person, [in] sports and otherwise. It was good. It starts real young. You're always learning. To this day I still have to be more disciplined with everything. You have a father figure there to help you out and give you opinions on things. He's been around a little bit longer than I have. He's getting pretty old. I'm always there listening to what he has to say and growing from it. It's always something I'm working on."

It's something he understood would help him on the field pretty early on. As easygoing as he may be, he's always been all business when it comes to baseball. He never knew how far he'd be able to go with the game, but he was certain of one thing from the outset: He wasn't going to let anything stand in his way of taking it as far as he could.

"I played football. I stopped when I went into high school. I realized that baseball was my main focus and football would've been a distraction. It would've been something fun to do, but it would've been a distraction from what really mattered," he said. "Baseball was my focus. It's like with anything. You do it, and you do it all out. That's how I took it."

Drennen undoubtedly dreamt of taking it all the way to the major leagues, but no one would ever confuse him with a head-in-the-clouds type. For that he has his mother to thank. Before thinking that John Sr. was solely responsible for shaping his son, realize that Barbie left a pretty big impression as well. "She was very easy to talk to. She had a bubbly personality," Smith, the scout, recalled. "She would call me to make sure I was coming on that day. It was an easy relationship to have right away."

"Being around your parents, you kind of get both personalities," Drennen added. My mom is real energetic, a real friendly person. She's a realist and that's kind of how I am. I'm not into all the BS. It is what it is."

Drennen headed to high school in the fall of 2001 armed with all of that wisdom. And it just wasn't any high school. Drennen attended the baseball paradise that is Rancho Bernardo High School. Michael Lewis, in *Moneyball*, details how in baseball circles the school was known simply as "The Factory" because of the vast numbers of professional prospects produced there. As a freshman Drennen played with Cole Hamels, taken seventeenth overall by the Phillies in the first round of the 2002 draft. He's now in Philadelphia's starting rotation. Jake Blalock was a senior that year as well, and the Phillies took him in the fifth round of that draft. Three years before Drennen got there, Jake's older brother Hank, a two-time American League All-Star third baseman with the Texas Rangers, was taken in the third round of the draft by Texas. (Blalock's uncle, Sam, is the coach at Rancho Bernardo and a San Diego coaching legend who also coached Oakland A's general manager Billy Beane.) In 2004 Danny Putnam—a player Drennen is often compared with—was taken by the A's with the thirty-sixth overall pick out of Stanford University, three years after leaving Rancho. Including Drennen, a total of six Broncos have been first-round selections in drafts over the years.

"Here's a kid who wasn't even a freshman when someone like [Hank] Blalock was there," Smith said. "I'm sure those guys came back and hit and hung out and gave these guys an idea of what professional baseball is all about. I think he just tried to take his game by looking at those guys as a measure."

Drennen, perhaps drawing on his mother's no-BS rule, never really got caught up in all the Rancho hype. All he cared about was going out and excelling between the white lines. "You're going out there and you're playing ball. You're not looking at it from that perspective [of worrying about who had gone to school there], at least not in my eyes," he said. "You're out here on a ball field. It's definitely nice knowing you're playing with a coach who knows what's going on and produced starters like that. You have Hank Blalock, Danny Putnam, and so on, but I never really looked at it in that way. I was just out there competing."

"I remember there being a lot of hype and commotion, a lot of stuff going on," he continued. "For the most part, there were always scouts coming around. There were always people saying stuff. I tried not to pay attention to all of it."

Rancho is a regular stop on the Southern California scouting trail, along with the other bigger high schools and colleges like UCLA, USC, Long Beach State, and Cal State-Fullerton. For Smith, an area scout since 1999 for the Indians, his first indelible memory of Drennen came in 2004 in a big area matchup against Mission Bay High School. Matt Bush, who would end up being taken as a shortstop with the first overall pick that June by the San Diego Padres, was on the mound that day.

"The kid had an advanced approach to hitting," said Smith, who remembered Drennen walking and singling against Bush. "You can tell at an early age. He had confidence in the box. He was always moving; he was always swinging the bat. He was the kind of athlete I looked for as far as, not necessarily a high-energy guy, but an energy guy. He always showed energy, confidence, and enthusiasm and it showed in his at bats."

"I do remember that well," Drennen said. "I played with [Bush] on a summer team. You always remember the guys who you faced. I think we beat them, 1–0. Not that it matters. I do remember playing Mission Bay and winning that game."

Drennen went on to play in the AFLAC All-American Game in the summer of 2004 with other top 2005 picks like Justin Upton (Diamondbacks, no. 1 overall), Cameron Maybin (Tigers, no. 10), Andrew McCutchen (Pirates, no. 11), Chris Volstad (Marlins, no. 16), C. J. Henry (Yankees, no. 17), and Beau Jones (Braves, no. 41). As a senior he hit .463 with 17 homers and was named State Player of the Year by Cal-Hi Sports. He finished his career with 47 home runs, a state record according to the Cal-Hi Sports record book.

Several teams were interested in Drennen and his power potential, including the Oakland A's. Under GM Billy Beane, they had taken Putnam the year earlier and Beane is undoubtedly up-to-date with what his former coach, Blalock, is up to. In the end, though, it was the Indians who took Drennen with their second pick in the 2005 draft, the thirty-third pick overall.

He had a decent, yet unspectacular debut in the summer of 2005, finishing the summer with a .238 average, albeit with 8 homers in fifty-one games for Burlington in the rookie-level Appalachian League. Sometimes, though, it pays to look deeper into the numbers to get the true sense of a player. The Indians were working with Drennen—a big-time pull hitter in high school—on hitting the ball to the opposite field. That, combined with the challenge of jumping from high school to pro ball, created problems for Drennen. On July 24, about a month into his pro career, he was hitting just .138. The Indians, while not pressing a panic button, were concerned enough to summon Smith, the scout who knew Drennen better than anyone, to see what was going on.

"As a scout the guys you first sign, every night you get online and you check the box scores," Smith said. "It drives you crazy, but you do it. I was worried a little bit.

"I was shocked [that he struggled in his pro debut]. I thought this kid would hit the ground running. He wouldn't spend long in rookie ball. I thought there was a chance he'd be moved up to Low-A. Those were my aspirations for him."

Normally, scouts will give players they've signed about a month before checking in on them. It was right after that thirty-day grace period that the Indians told Smith to head to Burlington to evaluate the situation. He watched Drennen take early batting practice, spoke at length with the manager and coaching staff, and tried to get a sense of what was going on with the teenager mentally. "They were trying to have him use the opposite field, take the ball the other way and drive it over the shortstop's head into the left-center gap. That's what he was having a hard time with. He had a hard time deciding which pitch to do it on. His strength really was to pull and show his power," Smith recalled.

Not long after Smith's visit, a light went on and Drennen started figuring out how to do what the Indians wanted. Smith remembers thinking when seeing that Drennen had homered to left-center field that, "he was going to click." Drennen hit .306 in August to raise his average 100 points over the final month to resurrect his season.

"The first initial thing was that the game sped up," Drennen said about the slow start. "You're no longer in your comfort zone. You're out of it. You're into something new and you have to adjust to it. That's what it comes down to, making adjustments. I felt like I adjusted well. You're getting used to a whole new team. It's something you go out and you take BP and you work on something and eventually it happens. I knew I was going to be successful. It's something I really worked on and I think I did a good job with it this year. There's always room to improve, but it's definitely coming along better."

It came along in a hurry during the 2006 season. Drennen went to full-season Lake County at age nineteen and began the year like everyone expected him to begin his career. He hit .333 over his first sixteen games before landing on the disabled list for a few weeks. After taking some time getting his rhythm back (he hit .270 in May), he got it going again in June, hitting .310 for the month. When the Captains traveled to Lexington for a four-game series beginning on June 5, Drennen was hitting .306. The power hadn't come yet—he had hit just three out with 15 RBIs heading into the series—but clearly Drennen was feeling pretty good about his swing.

On May 31, Drennen was working on a slightly different swing. The minor-league season, while twenty-two games shorter than that of the big leagues, is in many ways much more grueling. That's particularly true in the South Atlantic League, where very long bus rides are the norm. Before the meeting in Lexington, Drennen's Captains, whose Eastlake, Ohio, home is decidedly neither South nor Atlantic, had been on a whirlwind—but not uncommon—tour of Sally towns. On May 22, the Captains finished up a four-game series in Delmarva, Maryland. They returned home for four games against the Lakewood Blueclaws (according to Mapquest, that's an eight-hour ride). After four days at home, the Captains headed to Greensboro, North Carolina (another eight-hour trip). Four games later and the Lake County roster was back on the bus, headed back home to lose four straight to West Virginia (after one day off on the aforementioned May 31). There was no time to sulk following the sweep because the Captains had to head to Kentucky on a five and one-half hour trip for the fateful meeting with the Rocket.

On that off-day Drennen still didn't know about the matchup against Clemens. Like many professional baseball players, Drennen's time away from the field often meant time that could be spent on the golf course. Over the course of the eighteen holes, the conversation turned to major-league players doing rehab starts in the minor leagues. With the Captains' home just a stone's throw away from the parent club in Cleveland, it was fairly common for someone returning from injury to get some work in there under the watchful eye of the Indians. News of Clemens's signing was officially announced that day, so his name naturally came up.

"It just so happened one of the names we were talking about [was his]," Drennen recalled. "Later on that day, we heard we were going to face Clemens. It was cool; we had just had that conversation."

Before they could get to the excitement of facing a real legend, they had to face the Legends in game one of the four-game series on the heels of a five-game losing streak. To their credit they weren't looking ahead. Drennen hit a two-run double in the seventh to give Lake County a lead they would then relinquish in the bottom of the inning. But the Captains scored twice in the top of the ninth to snap their losing streak and send them into the "Clemens game" with some renewed confidence.

The game on June 6 started just as one would expect with a guy who had 300-plus big-league wins under his belt facing a bunch of kids: with a strikeout. Lake County leadoff hitter Niuman Romero, who was born in 1985, Clemens's second year with the Red Sox, was caught looking. Marshall Szabo, the number two hitter and 2004 draft pick, grounded out to second. That brought up Drennen, who tried to play this day as though it was just another game.

"I was looking forward to it, to the opportunity," Drennen admitted. "It'll probably be the only time I'll get to face him. I was definitely excited. He's a Hall of Famer. But I pretty much went about it the way I was always going about it. There was a little bit more adrenaline going, that's for sure. It was an awesome experience. I know the guys on the team were excited and I was excited, but I tried to go about it the same way. You take the same approach. You're facing a guy and you're competing. You hope you see something and get a good swing on it, you know, take a hack."

Trying hard to take the same approach, Drennen strode to the plate with two outs and nobody on.

Clemens fed Drennen some split-fingered fastballs out of the strike zone. Drennen swung and missed the first one. He fouled a fastball straight back to fall behind 0–2. Clemens went back to the split, throwing one away in the dirt, but Drennen "had seen it, I had kind of recognized it, so I was laying off of it." A fastball out of the zone evened the count 2–2.

Thousands of hitters had been in this position before, facing Roger Clemens with two strikes. It's not generally a good place to be, not against a guy who is second all-time in strikeouts. That didn't seem to faze Drennen, even though, as ESPN commentator Harold Reynolds said after the game, "He starts getting into off-speed pitches they've never seen before, that's when you get into trouble."

"It just so happens Clemens threw me the splitty at 2–2," Drennen said. "And I hit it out."

While Drennen may have been working on hitting the ball the other way since joining the organization, he turned on the splitter Clemens hung and hit it out to right. Drennen knew he had hit it well, but he also knew that the sentence for a teenager standing and watching the flight of a shot hit off of Roger Clemens would be one under the chin later on, either to him or one of his teammates. "I know I put a good swing on it. I knew who I was facing on the mound. I wasn't going to show anybody up. I just hit it and ran fast," Drennen said. "Probably somewhere around first base, I got that kind of look on my face. I was definitely jacked. It was a great feeling. One of the better moments I've had. Everyone was giving me the fists and high fives and all the things that come with it. They were all saying, 'You're going to be on ESPN tonight.' I remember coming home and that was all over the place. It was cool."

Clemens was certainly gracious afterward, having some fun with the experience. While with the Captains, Drennen wore number 22. That just so happens to be Clemens's jersey number, so the Rocket tried to portray the hung splitter as a favor from one "22" to another. "I was thinking that he had a great number, so I'd hang him a split," joked Clemens. "He did what he's supposed to do with splits that are up there. He hit it. I'll have to ask him how that room service was."

It looked for a moment that Clemens had quite a bit of rust to shake off. The following batter, Matt Fornasiere—also a 2005 draftee—doubled to center. But Clemens settled down, striking out three of the next four batters. In the top of the third, though, he gave up an infield single to Juan Valdes, a stolen base, and a hit-by-pitch (Marshall Szabo). That brought Drennen up for a second shot at Clemens, this time with one out and two men aboard. If the first inning was storybook, at bat number two was more according to the expected script. Clemens stuck with fastballs away and made Drennen look, well, like a teenager just starting to play the game. "My second at bat I had a terrible approach," Drennen recounted. "I had a feeling for some reason that he was going to come in and hard on me. But he stayed out and away. I just took a terrible swing. It wasn't a good at-bat. It's the kind of at bat that jumps out at you and makes you realize you're young."

Both Drennen and Fornasiere struck out swinging to end the inning and Clemens's outing. He threw sixty-two pitches over three innings of work, yielding 3 hits and a run on Drennen's homer, while striking out 6. Drennen didn't get the chance to discuss his moment with Clemens directly, but the hurler did take some time out to address all of the Captains during his stay in Lexington.

"He came to talk to us about hard work, loving the game, and picking your spots, to be smart and stay out of trouble," Drennen said. "It was definitely nice to hear from a guy who's been around. I definitely respect that. You definitely listened to what he had to say because he's been there and had so much success. I definitely understood where he was coming from. It definitely takes hard work and you have to separate yourself from the distractions. You have to really bear down."

Just like the previous June, the first Tuesday of the month was day one of Major League Baseball's First-Year Player Draft. The Indians scouts, like the staffs of big-league organizations around baseball, had congregated in their "war room" at home, in this case, Cleveland. Once the draft was done for the day, attention turned to see how the affiliate would do down in Lexington against Clemens. One scout in particular was extremely interested to see how his top signee fared.

"We were in the draft room," Smith said. "We were all sitting in a conference room watching and we all went crazy when he hit it. I called his dad right

away. He was at a business meeting... I said, 'Hey
John, Jason Smith.' He said, 'Hey Jason, how are you
doing?' I said, 'You're not going to believe this. Your
son just hit a home run off of Roger Clemens.' He
thought I was joking. 'Get out of here,' he said. 'Are
you playing a practical joke on me?' He couldn't believe it. He was really excited. Then his mom called
me right after that. That was Johnny's moment. I let
him have it. I didn't want to make it seem like I was
following the kid's every move. I let him have the moment and enjoy it and move on. I didn't end up talking to him about it until a month or so later."

That month may have been a bit of a blur for Drennen. The homer had extended his hit streak to five
games, a stretch that hit seven before being snapped a
few days later. He went deep the following day and finished June with four round-trippers, a high for him in
his first full season. He appeared in the South Atlantic
League All-Star Game, held in his home park in Eastlake, as a reserve, near the end of the month. He went
on a tear in July, hitting .356 over sixteen games before
getting promoted to Class-A Advanced Kinston. Maybe
it's the state of North Carolina, but Drennen struggled
with that move much like he did when he headed to
Burlington after he signed a year earlier. After hitting
.297 over his first ten games, he hit .224 in August and
finished with a .239 average in thirty-one games. His
OPS (on base + slugging percentage), which was .880
in Lake County, fell to .656 in Kinston. The K-Tribe
went on to win the Carolina League championship, but
Drennen would see action in just two playoff games,
going 2 for 7 in his limited appearances.

"The main thing for me is to not really think and just play the game," Drennen said. "When I first got there, there was so much information coming. I was trying to figure it out instead of just playing the game. You swing the stick and play the game and play hard. You know what you do and you do it.

"In Lake County I did that for the most part [until] I got called up. That's what kind of progressed. A lot more information was coming then and I wasn't really playing the game. I kind of got out of it. That's what I need to work on more consistently."

Even with the struggles in Kinston, Drennen's first full season was certainly a success. He finished with a combined .295 average and .384 on-base percentage in ninety-eight games. He made it to High-A ball at age nineteen. By every measure he's still very much ahead of the curve.

And that's not just for his play on the field. Because of his moment against Clemens, Drennen had to take a crash course on what media attention was like. After being on just about every highlight film under the sun, Drennen was a pretty popular guy with local and national reporters alike. So while he was still shagging flies and taking extra BP, he also had to sharpen skills that often go untouched, at least during the early stages of a prospect's rise through the minors.

"It was definitely a good experience, a good learning experience," Drennen said about the series of interviews he did following his home run. "Getting to speak to the media and getting comfortable with that, it's definitely a learning process. You learn from each interview and get more comfortable with each one. It's all about a comfort level, learning to get rid of the 'umms.' You are who you are, but you have to work on those things. I look back at doing all those interviews and realize it was kind of nice, but I'm definitely still the same person."

"He takes it in stride. He has a pretty clear head," Smith agreed. "He's able to enjoy the moment and move on to his next at bat. Maybe on the inside he was really enjoying it. But he's a professional kid, a businesslike kid. He was able to enjoy the moment and move on, I think."

Drennen may say he's the same person, but that's not entirely accurate. Before going deep against the Rocket, he was known as John Drennen. That day in Lexington, however, he was called Johnny, perhaps a subconscious attempt to separate the man (Clemens) from the boys. Little did he know that would be the nomenclature he would carry into history. Relying on that surfer attitude a bit, Drennen is none too concerned about circumstances forever changing how he is greeted.

"A name is a name. You call me Johnny, however you want to say it. It really doesn't matter," he said. "I like Johnny now, if it sticks. You are who you are and you know where you came from, and that doesn't change. You really have to be a little kid to do everything, so I'll stick to Johnny. John sounded a little bit [grown up]. I have to keep the little kid in me."

There are almost no sure things in baseball. Such a minute percentage of all players who enter pro ball get to the ultimate goal of playing in the big leagues.

The odds are astronomical for anyone, even a first-round pick like Johnny Drennen. It does seem, though, that he possesses the right mix of on-field skills and off-the-field attitude to overcome those odds. He's drawn several comparisons to other players with excellent track records of big-league success. Early on, he looked like a young Mark Kotsay. Some say he'll eventually develop into a player like Brian Giles, a former San Diego high school standout. And his left-handed swing bears an uncanny resemblance to fellow Rancho grad Hank Blalock's. It certainly will be interesting to see if Drennen can live up to those comparisons over time.

If he doesn't, he still has something he can hang his hat on. It may seem like just an answer to a future trivia question, but even if Drennen never spends a day in the major leagues, no one can take that one swing away from him. He will forever be etched in baseball history for taking Roger Clemens out of the ballpark in Lexington on that June night.

"It's part of the game. It's fine. I had a good time with it," Drennen said about being known for the one home run. "It's something you can look back on and say it was a part of my career. I still have a few things I want to accomplish. I want to keep getting better. But it's something that happened and something that will always stay in my memory."

KOBY **CLEMENS**

THERE'S A SCENE IN THE BASEBALL comedy *Major League* when the hated Yankees bring in intimidating relief pitcher Duke Temple. Broadcaster Harry Doyle, played by Bob Uecker, proclaims, "This guy threw at his own son in a father-son game." Cue laughter.

Sometimes life imitates *art,* though using the term art to describe that film might be pushing things a bit. That's certainly what everyone thought was going on when Roger Clemens apparently brushed back his son, Koby, at the Houston Astros Spring Training facility in late February of 2006. The youngster, a 2005 draftee of the Astros, homered off of his father in his first at bat of a simulated game and, as the legend would have you believe, the elder Clemens wanted to make sure everyone knew who was boss.

It's time to set the record straight. Yes, Roger did come up and in during Koby's second plate appearance. No, the "victim" insists, Dad wasn't trying to knock his eldest son down. "I know if my dad wanted to hit me, he would've smoked me," Koby Clemens laughed. "He's dusted me a couple of times. I just think he was trying to bust me in, trying to jam me, thinking I was going to try and get extended so I could hit another one out."

Well, that's comforting. The legend of the purpose pitch might be too large to overcome, but here is what actually happened, at least according to the younger Clemens involved. Koby was in his first Spring Training as part of the Astros organization, having been Houston's eighth-round draft pick the previous June. His father was still unofficially retired, in camp solely to get into shape for the upcoming World Baseball Classic.

Koby and fellow minor leaguers Tommy Manzella and Neil Sellers were going through a few rounds of batting practice while Roger was warming up. Then the elder Clemens did something his son has seen him do many times in recent years as the pair engaged in countless father-son battles. "He moved the 'L' screen out of the way and said, 'OK, we're going to go full out. Game on,'" Koby recalled. "I think he had a three-inning simulated game. I said, 'OK, who's leading us off.' Tommy said, 'You lead off. It's your dad.'"

Koby dug in for his first at bat, thinking first-pitch fastball. "If it's somewhere in my happy zone, I'm going to get into it. He threw a first-pitch fastball, it was in my happy zone, and I hit it. I was kind of worried because it looked bad, especially on TV, because I hit it—we had decided that if you put a ball in play, you were supposed to get out of there and let the next guy in. I knew I had hit it good, but I didn't think it was going to get out. It almost looked like I did a right-handed Griffey down the third-base line, like I hit it and started walking down the line. I promise, that's not what I was trying to do. I was just trying to get out of the box so Tommy could get in. Then it went over by a good amount and the camera crews started chuckling, saying 'Oooo.' My dad said, 'Really, right out the gate, huh?' "

After Manzella and Sellers took their first turns, it was time for the nineteen-year-old Clemens to get in the box again. He took a first-pitch slider on the outside corner for a strike. Then Roger came back with a two-seamer that rose up and in, forcing Koby to pull back to get out of the way. A legend was born and Koby knew right away it was going to be a big deal. "Immediately in my head, I was thinking, 'The media's going to take this and run with it. After I hit a bomb, they're going to go crazy with this,' " he said. "I then proceeded to strike out looking on a slider away. He just embarrassed me with the next at bat. I want to say I was 2 for 4 or 2 for 5 against him, so I was happy. My dad was just laughing."

It wasn't the first time the son had taken his father deep. Maybe it was the first time he did so with the media watching, but the competitive father and son were no strangers to going at it full tilt. "I've hit a few home runs off of him. I don't know about first pitch. I did it again this 2007 Spring Training," Koby said. "I've faced my dad so many times. There've been times I've hit one good and he's hit me in the butt or something like that. Not a hard fastball, but he'd say, 'Quit looking at it.' It's usually after I've hit one good and I stare at it like I'm something bad. He's plunked me a few times, but there's also been some times I've hit some comebackers that have smoked him in the ribcage. I've gotten my fair payback."

Koby Clemens has never known his father to be anything other than a major-league superstar. The first of four Clemens boys (all with names beginning, shockingly, with the letter K: Koby, Kory, Kacy, and Kody) was born in December of 1986, just a couple of months after Clemens's dominant Cy Young and MVP season ended with the loss in the World Series in seven games to the Mets. As a result, what may not seem routine for most people was just that for the Clemens kids, especially the two eldest: Koby and Kory, who was born about a year and half after Koby. Dad was around a lot during the off-season, but once it was time for pitchers and catchers to report, they were used to the fact they wouldn't see much of him for the next several months.

"Me and my brother Kory, we never had a problem with my dad being gone," Koby said. "When we were born, he was doing his thing. We just got accustomed to him being gone all the time and talking to him on the phone every night. I never had a problem with it. Obviously, I had wished he could be there for more games, more than normal. You'd see the other dads there videotaping and all that. But my dad was always up on the scoop on everything we were doing."

It's not that they wouldn't be able to catch up in person at all. Once summer hit, there would be visits to Boston with Koby and Kory making themselves feel right at home at the ballpark, starting in Fenway Park's less-than-spacious home clubhouse. "I have vague memories of running through the Red Sox clubhouse and on the field. I've got a bunch of videotapes of us doing the Green Monsters versus mini-Fenway fellows, the father-son games," said Koby, and no, the Rocket didn't plunk his son in those contests. "I got to meet Mo Vaughn and some other players from back then. In Toronto I got to run around the clubhouse a little bit. I didn't think too much of it, until probably he was in New York, I kind of realized what they were doing and I stayed out of their way.

"I'm very blessed I've gotten the opportunity, through all the stuff my dad's done, to be around those big-league players. My brothers and I have been running around clubhouses for a long time."

They did it because that's what the Clemens family would do during the summer. It was their norm and it seems as though Roger and Debbie Clemens tried not to make too big a deal about who Dad was when the kids were younger. Obviously, they knew something was a little different, but at the same time, whenever the best right-hander in the game came home after a season, there wasn't any question who he was. Koby never had one of those "Aha!" moments, suddenly discovering his father's fame, though as he got older and began to develop a greater appreciation of the game of baseball, he did recognize that not every big leaguer was like his dad.

"It never clicked like that," he explained. "Off the field and on the field, he's always been just Dad. I guess it really sunk in just how great he was on the field, I was probably eleven or twelve years old when I realized that the things he was doing were not the things the average major-league player does. That's when it just wowed me. Off the field he's never changed to me. At home, with him, whenever we do anything, working out or whatever, he's always just Dad to me, just like anybody else."

That sounds like it would be a tough sell to his friends and peers, but, for the most part, they took the fact their buddy was a Clemens in stride. There were some times when he first got to high school when it became a small issue. He switched from private to public school and there was the initial "Oh, you're Roger Clemens's son" reaction.

It was, in many ways, the first time Koby had to "face" his dad, or at least the specter of his fame. That wasn't easy for Koby, who was shy and nervous around other people when he first met them. But all it took was a trip to the Clemens household during the off-season to realize, as Crash Davis tells Nuke in *Bull Durham* when the phenom's father is in the stands, that Dad is just as full of sh-- as the rest of us. The elder Clemens embraces that by simply enjoying being with his sons and their friends. The younger did his part by not having any big-league attitude about his last name.

"The best thing people have said is that if I didn't have the last name on my jersey, they wouldn't know I was a Clemens. I'm just like any other kid," Koby said. "When I started hanging around with some of the kids on the football team in middle school, I had a couple of them over to the house. Once they got to meet my dad, once they talked to him and saw how goofy he is, how sociable and easy to talk to he is, they liked him just like any other dad. They'd forget about everything he's done and the stardom he has. They'd throw jokes at each other. He has a good relationship with the friends that I have."

It's understandable that there would be an initial hesitation in meeting Roger Clemens, even off the field. The only persona the outside public has to go by is the one Clemens has on the mound. It would not be surprising if Koby's friends thought of the hard fastball, the glare from atop the pitching rubber, and the willingness to pitch inside and translated it into some vision of a hard-assed father who was downright ornery. *Goofy* is not a word one would ever use to describe Roger Clemens at work. Then again, he wouldn't be the first person who acts very different at the office than he does at home.

"When he's on the mound, he's very intimidating," Koby said, knowingly. "When he's up there and he's ready, and he's boxed in on you at the plate, it makes you get nervous in the box. A lot of people take that, and see all that he does on the field, his aggressiveness and how emotionally he gets into games, how fired up and pumped up he gets, they think he's this intense guy 24/7. The real thing is, when he gets off the field and gets home, even if he's had a bad game, about an hour after he's gotten home, he's back to normal and he's like a goofy three-year-old."

Before that starts sounding like just cause for some more chin music at the next father-son meeting, Clemens is quick to continue, saying that whenever a kid-like, fun-loving attitude is needed—from the backyard, when the pair dress up in football uniforms just

to be silly, to an amusement park, when Roger is likely
to be clamoring to get on the cool rides first—his father always steps up and comes through like it's a
huge start in the middle of a pennant race.

"I'm not saying that in a bad way," Koby said.
"He's a fun guy. Now that I'm getting older, my dad
and I are getting a lot closer. I'm going through a lot
of the things he's gone through, so I've got more understanding of how hard it is to get to the major-
league level. It's not as much a father-son relationship
anymore, it's a friend-to-friend relationship. We goof
around, joke about stuff. He knows how to make everything so much more fun. It's the thing I love about
him most. He wants us to have fun, but he's a big
kid, too."

People looking for the *E! True Hollywood
Story* on the Clemens family will have to look elsewhere. There are no sordid tales about baseball
player's kids running amok, wreaking havoc. Sure,
Koby became friends with some of his father's
teammates' kids while running around those clubhouses and elsewhere—they did share an understanding of what life as a ballplayer's son was
like—but they weren't the only relationships the
young third baseman had, likely something much
healthier for everyone involved.

"I know a lot of the big-leaguers' children that
live in my area, like the Drabeks," Koby said, refer-
ring to Doug Drabek, the former Cy Young Award
winner who had a thirteen-year career mostly with
the Pittsburgh Pirates and Houston Astros. "Their
son Kyle is doing his thing now [he was a 2006

first-round pick of the Philadelphia Phillies] and we grew up playing baseball together.

"I've had friends in the baseball community, but I also have plenty of my own friends. There's never been any problems worrying that there are people around me only because of my dad. They know me for me. They trust me and I trust them."

One of the better bonuses of growing up a big-league legend's son is feeling comfortable in a major-league setting. Other young minor-league players might show up for their first Spring Training and be in awe of their surroundings, not sure how to act around the superstars in camp. That's never been an issue for Koby Clemens. With everything his father has done in the game, he's gotten to meet and be-friend some of the biggest names the game has ever seen. He met Mr. October, Reggie Jackson, during his dad's first tour with the Yankees. He grew up with the B&B boys—Jeff Bagwell and Craig Biggio—both of whom could end up in Cooperstown alongside Roger, in Houston. They've become close family friends over the years. The only big name that really stopped Clemens in his tracks was Fox, and it wasn't Nellie.

"Everybody asks me if I get star struck when I'm around big-league players and I don't, really," Koby said. "I guess I've grown up around them my whole life. I'm kind of used to the players. There's a very good comfort level. The only time I ever remember being starstruck was when I met Michael J. Fox last year at Disney. I almost couldn't speak because I love all the movies he's done."

Another fact that runs counter to the idea of Roger Clemens being an intimidating, domineering parent is that he never once tried to force Koby, or any of his kids, into following in his enormous footsteps. He also didn't try to dissuade any of his sons from taking the ball either. To his credit the elder Clemens has always tried to let his children find their own way on the field.

Koby did, on occasion, dabble with pitching. But he knew right away it wasn't his calling. When he was eight years old, Koby played in one of those leagues where everyone on the team gets to pitch an inning or two. By this time his father had been in the big leagues for about a decade and had taken home three Cy Young Awards. Rest assured, there was some eager anticipation when Rocket offspring number one took the hill for the first time. But while there may have been some buzz around Koby Clemens, it wasn't something he felt internally. He had fared just fine—if there's one thing a Clemens knows, it's how to compete at any level—but he wasn't hooked by any kind of pitching rush.

"After the game, I said, 'You know, Dad, I didn't really enjoy doing that too much.' I liked playing defense and worrying about hitting, I guess," Koby said. "He never pushed me to pitch and he never pushed me away from pitching."

While his brothers have all pitched at various stages, Koby managed to stay off the mound from that day of Little League until deep into his high school career. Then he had to help out a summer team in relief because it had run out of pitching. His high school coach saw the outing and his eyes lit up. "My high school coach was watching and he told me, 'You get ready to pitch next season,'" Clemens said. "That's the only time I really pitched: my junior and senior year of high school."

Not surprisingly, he pitched pretty well and opened the eyes of some scouts. It would have been hard to completely disregard his results on the mound. In his final year of high school, he was able to crank his fastball up into the 90s and tossed two no-hitters. As impressive as that was, most agreed that this Clemens's future would be at third base and in the batter's box, not on the mound.

He has a swing honed over time by countless pitches and tips from his father. That by itself is not a new story, but there aren't too many young hitters who can work on their craft by hitting off one of the greatest pitchers of all time. Obviously, it's not like Roger started firing mid-90s fastballs at his son as he was learning how to walk. Just like the father-son relationship Koby said has evolved into more of a friendship, so has their pitcher-hitter rapport changed over time.

It started when Koby was about four years old and Dad would flip balls to his son and it's grown from there as father would help son develop his swing. Now, when the elder Clemens needs to throw a bullpen session, he just tells his son to grab a bat and take some swings. The big-league pitcher gets his work in while helping his son improve as a hitter. Roger would always make sure it was challenging enough for Koby, for sure, but the gloves didn't truly come off until Koby was fifteen years old.

It was the summer of 2002, Clemens's fourth season wearing Yankee pinstripes. He had won titles
with New York in 1999 and 2000 and lost the World
Series in 2001 to the Diamondbacks. At various points
in his Yankee career, though, Clemens dealt with
some leg injuries. In 1999, a season that saw his ERA
climb to 4.60, he had a hamstring problem. In 2000
he struggled in the first part of the season, hit the DL
in mid-June with a groin injury, then came back better than ever, going 9–0 with a 2.21 ERA over fifteen
starts down the stretch. In 2001 his legs held up and,
not surprisingly, won his sixth Cy Young Award.

He had more problems in 2002, when another
groin injury forced him back onto the disabled list in
July. That might have been tough for Yankee fans,
but it was great for Koby Clemens. While he would
be able to spend some time with his father and whatever team he was on in the clubhouse most summers,
he normally wouldn't have two weeks of solid father-
son time. But Koby got to head to Tampa to hang
out, and work out, with Roger for two weeks. It
turned out be a fantasy camp of sorts for Koby, who
was given the opportunity to participate in an extended Spring Training program with Yankee minor
leaguers. From time to time over the course of the
two-week stint, Koby jumped in on some groups with
players like Juan Rivera, who was just starting to establish himself as a big leaguer.

At that point Roger was preparing to throw a
simulated game and his son was allowed to be one of
the hitters he faced. It was the first time Koby had
ever really tried to hit with his father going full tilt. "I

used a wooden bat in my first two at bats and I struck out both times," Koby recalled. "I grounded out in my next one, then I got my metal bat and I struck out again. The metal didn't help me whatsoever. You still have to make contact. I just remember saying, 'Wow.' It was like he threw on a different switch. I didn't feel too bad because the other guys weren't hitting too well, either. I was definitely overmatched at fifteen."

That was just the beginning of a head-to-head contest that is still on-going. It didn't matter if Roger Clemens was a Yankee, an Astro, a Yankee again, or in retirement. Not one to stay still, Roger was always keeping in shape, even if he wasn't sure he'd be pitching competitively again. Dad would make sure his son came along for the ride, keeping up with him every step of the way.

One of the amazing things about the elder Clemens has been the overall health of his arm. His legs may not have cooperated as much, but his arm strength at his age is nearing superhero status. Case in point: In the last two years, when he thought he wasn't coming back, he'd throw batting practice for an hour at a time—all arm—without any repercussions. Then Koby would hear those words: "Full out. Game on," and that meant it was time to ratchet up the intensity level a few notches. That usually included a steady stream of good-natured trash talking and would often draw a Clemens family crowd to watch.

"I've done this so many times against him, I'm comfortable with it, with him going full out and me going full out," Koby said. "He'd get me and say,

'That's right. Father Time's still got it.' Then in my next at bat, I'll hit one good right up the middle, right past his head, and I'll say, 'You're getting a little older. I don't want that ball to come back and break your hip or something.' We'll just jaw at each other. It's fun. My mom comes out there, she's trying to make sure everything's OK. My two younger brothers, Kacy and Kody, they're cheering it on. It's a lot of fun. I must have had 200, maybe 300 at bats, going full-out like that, in the past five years of my life."

Roger Clemens has never been one to allow a whole lot of base hits, keeping his career batting average against mark under .230. So it's not difficult to imagine that the younger Clemens probably didn't scratch out too many over the course of those one-on-one meetings. Koby does seem to enjoy the spotlight, perhaps a sign of being able to step up in pressure situations in the future. And it's not because his dad lets up or goes easy on him. When Koby digs in, he knows he can't always look first-pitch fastball like he did back in the spring of 2006. "I'm not going to say it's too good," Koby said about his career batting average against his father. "I will say when the cameras show up, I'm hitting well against him then. Whenever cameras have shown up, I've done something big against him.

"But he's broken a lot of my bats, with two-seamers in, and he'll say, 'That's right. Can't get those hands out there.' He'll drop the splitter on you anytime, anywhere. The worst thing is, it's sitting in the back of your mind, is he going to throw the splitter here, and you take a fastball right down the middle."

Before the 2004 season, these kinds of battles, this evolution of their relationship, could only really take place during the off-season. But then Roger Clemens decided to come home, signing with the Houston Astros. That enabled Koby and the K boys to see a lot more of their dad. He, in turn, was around in a way Koby and Kory had never experienced.

"When he came to Houston and started playing for the Astros, my dad got to see a lot more of my last year of high school and my first season of pro ball," Koby said. "He's always proud of me, no matter what I do. But when he came to my games, I almost always played better because I wanted to perform that much more to make him proud."

Roger was undoubtedly proud in June of 2005 when, in his second season pitching for the Astros—en route to Cy Young Award number seven—his team selected his son in the eighth round of the draft. Some saw it as a "favor pick," especially since word on the street was that Koby was going to follow in his father's footsteps by attending the University of Texas. But those kinds of favor picks usually don't happen early in the draft and the Astros were intent on bringing the young third baseman into the fold. As it turned out, Koby Clemens was more than happy to comply. Having his father with the Astros, he says, did not affect his decision. He didn't sign because Roger Clemens was an Astro. But he thinks that connection certainly helped the Astros realize up close what kind of player Koby could be.

"I think him playing there had a big part in Houston getting to see me and what my capabilities were,"

Koby agreed. "They got an up close tour of me without any problems. During the season I'd come up there and hit BP regularly. I'd take ground balls with Morgan Ensberg. I'd hit in the pitchers group before everyone else was out there and I was hitting them in the Crawford Boxes [at Minute Maid Park] like it was nothing.

"They got to see me for a whole year before the draft. I think that's what made their decision to pick me. That's what sold them. For me it came down to starting now. If I was in college, I'd be about to become a junior. If I was drafted next year, I'd be starting rookie ball or the New York-Penn League. I'm kind of ahead of that pace right now."

Not that the ultracompetitive Clemens doesn't want to move faster. Dealing with some injuries in his first full season slowed him down some and he was forced to spend a second year with Lexington in the Low-A South Atlantic League. Having a father with more than two decades of experience in the business certainly helps, but only to an extent. He may have plenty of insight into dealing with the peaks and valleys of a long baseball season, but considering he spent a total of seventeen games in the minor leagues before reaching Boston back in 1984, his knowledge of surviving minor-league life might be a little lacking.

"Luckily, I have my dad to keep me level-headed and to keep my confidence up," Clemens said. "He knows exactly how it's going. He's been around for twenty-three years. He understands what I'm going through when I tell him about the stuff I'm going through.

"He was in and out [of the minors] real quick, but he was older. College pitchers are usually the ones who move to the big leagues the quickest. I always joke with him about that as well, about being in the minors. He'll say, 'I know what it's like for you.' I'll tell him, 'Dad, you have no idea what it's like in the minors.' This is my second full season and I'm in Lexington, which probably has the longest bus trips of anyone in the country. I just made a trip to play the BlueClaws and it was a fourteen-hour drive, so I don't want to hear it."

They did share one minor-league moment and it's one that will certainly last a lifetime. Roger Clemens decided late in 2006 to come back for one more season with the Houston Astros. Although he was in pretty good shape, partly because that's who he is and partly because he had been throwing for the World Baseball Classic, he couldn't step right into the Astros rotation after deciding to come back in late May. He had, after all, thought he was pitching in the Classic and then going home. So he embarked on a minor-league tour, with three stops geared toward getting him ready to pitch once again in the big leagues.

The first stop on the Houston organizational ladder was its lowest full-season level club, the Lexington Legends of the South Atlantic League. The Legends third baseman, of course, was none other than Koby Clemens. A year after he was drafted—June 6, 2006—the younger Clemens was able to wear the same uniform and play on the same team as his father in a competitive setting. All those years, all those one-on-one matchups, came to a climax when

Koby was able hand the ball to his father to start the game against the Lake County Captains.

In the final frame of Roger's three-inning stint, his son brought the ball to him. Dad thought son was bringing a scouting report for the South Atlantic League hitters he'd be facing. Instead, he told him that he needed just 1 more strikeout to get to 5 for the game. If he did that, his son explained, everyone in the crowd would get free washer fluid. Roger struck out 2 to finish with 6, sending everyone home with much cleaner windshields. (Ever the populist, Roger went on to pitch for Double-A Corpus Christi and struck out enough players to earn everyone in attendance free taquitos, courtesy of the stadium sponsor, Whataburger.)

With his father's age and his own distance from the big leagues in mind, Koby Clemens knew quite well that probably was it in terms of him sharing a professional field with his father. Considering the atmosphere in Lexington that night, with 9,222 crammed into Applebee's Park, the eldest son of Roger Clemens doesn't mind that one bit. "It probably was the best game I've ever played in my life. The most memorable, without a doubt," Koby said. "I think it hit me more after the game was over. During the game I was just ready to play and focusing on that. It was cool, going full out with my pops on the mound. Not many people have gotten to play with their fathers. The Griffeys did it. I'm blessed I got to do it in the minor leagues.

"It's a long shot—my dad is on his way out of baseball—I don't think I've got a shot [at playing with him in the big leagues]. I'm still young, trying to mature and get ready for the big leagues. I'm only twenty years old, trying to work my way up. It was an experience of a lifetime. It felt like a major-league game because our stadium was packed. People were on top of people at the game. It was loud, crazy, awesome. When that first pitch was thrown with all the flashes, I felt like it was at the World Series back in 2003, with my dad's last start."

Of course that World Series outing was the first of several "last starts" for Koby's dad. Who knows, maybe he can stick around long enough to play in a big-league stadium with his son, though that does indeed seem unlikely. Unselfishly, Koby thinks about his father's eventual retirement and how good it will be for his younger brothers, Kacy and Kody. Without an ounce of bitterness or regret, Koby knows they will benefit from something he and his brother Kory didn't get while their dad was putting up Hall of Fame numbers.

"I think he's on his way out, even though he's still doing his thing now," Koby said. "He'll be able to see them play a lot more, see them play football, basketball, and baseball. He's going to be around and it's going to mean so much to them that he's around."

When exactly he's going to start being around is a question Koby doesn't exactly know the answer to. Being a member of the family, being the oldest of four boys, doesn't automatically guarantee knowledge of the career plans of Roger Clemens. Koby has seen his father at the end of seasons, worn out from the amount of work it takes for him to be, well, Roger

Clemens, and thought that was finally it. Then the calendar page would turn, talk would turn to pitchers and catchers reporting, and his dad, always keeping in shape regardless of what the future seemed to hold, would start getting the itch to get on the mound and compete. That meant more than simply going "full out" against his son, which is why Koby cannot begin to honestly predict when his father will actually call it a career.

"He loves going out there and competing. It's not like he goes out there and gets ripped apart. He goes out there and deals," Koby said with admiration. "He's still got a lot of confidence. He's got a ton of confidence in himself competing, but I don't think he's got as much confidence in his body. It's not his arm. It's his lower body. His lower half may not be keeping up, but you don't see too many forty-five-year-olds getting up and doing what he's doing.

"If I were a betting man, I don't even know," Koby Clemens said. "If I were a betting man, I'd have to say he's done after this year. Then again, I said that last year and the year before that."

INDEX